William Black

Lady Silverdale's Sweetheart

And Other Tales

William Black

Lady Silverdale's Sweetheart
And Other Tales

ISBN/EAN: 9783744676335

Printed in Europe, USA, Canada, Australia, Japan

Cover: Foto ©Thomas Meinert / pixelio.de

More available books at **www.hansebooks.com**

LADY SILVERDALE'S SWEETHEART

AND OTHER TALES

BY

WILLIAM BLACK

NEW AND REVISED EDITION

LONDON

SAMPSON LOW, MARSTON & COMPANY
LIMITED

St. Dunstan's House

1892

LONDON :

PRINTED BY WILLIAM CLOWES AND SONS, LIMITED,
STAMFORD STREET AND CHARING CROSS.

CONTENTS.

LADY SILVERDALE'S SWEETHEART.

B

LADY SILVERDALE'S SWEETHEART.

CHAPTER I.

FIVE-AND-THIRTY.

A BRIGHT, mild, and genial day in February; a frail sunshine glimmering through the thin blue mist hanging about St. James's Park; the light catching here and there on the lake, and the green shrubs, and the yellow piebald bark of the plane-trees—suggesting, altogether, one of Corot's tender, shadowy, spectral landscapes. A lady and her son were walking briskly along the Mall—it was a day that invited even the aged and infirm out of doors. This lady wore a tight-fitting grey Ulster coat, a Rubens hat, and a standing-up collar; but although there was enough that was "mannish" in her attire, there was nothing of the kind in the expression of her face, which was singularly refined, and even beautiful. She had pale, fine features; large grey eyes, full

B 2

of brilliancy, under dark lashes; she had beautifully cut lips, perhaps looking all the redder for the paleness of her face; and she had abundant masses of golden hair, tightly braided under that picturesque hat. This was Lady Silverdale. She was thirty-five years of age; with her slender figure, her erect carriage, and the bright cheerfulness of her face, she did not look more than twenty.

She was walking hand-in-hand with a small boy of eight or nine, who had eyes like her own, but whose hair, flowing down on his shoulders, was even lighter than hers. She was carrying a small parcel which she had purchased in St. James's Street.

"Harry," she said to him, as they got opposite Buckingham Palace, "do you remember your Uncle Frank?"

"A little, mamma."

"He is coming back to England now; and he will come and see you; and you must tell him how glad you are to have your dear uncle back again."

"I am not glad, mamma; and I hope he won't come and see us," said the young gentleman frankly.

" Why ? "

" Because he is a bad man, that wants to kill the Queen, and give our house, and my pony, and all that we have away to the beggars."

The mother looked amazed.

" Whoever put such nonsense into your head, child ? " she demanded.

" Maudey read it in the newspapers," said he.

" Maudey must have been making fun. Maudey has no business to read the newspapers, and talk about what she does not understand. I suppose she was giving you lessons in politics. Now mind, Harry, when your Uncle Frank comes to see you, you must be very kind to him, and love him very much, and you must forget all that silly nonsense that Maudey has put into your head."

Harry received these instructions with meek obedience ; but he was not convinced. This Uncle Frank—who was really a cousin of Lady Silverdale's, but had received a courtesy title from the children—had been away from England for something like two years and a half ; and Harry had no particular remembrance of his many acts of kindness. On the other hand, the loyal young Englishman was determined, before he quite made friends with his home-coming uncle, to receive a distinct assurance that he had never meant to kill the Queen or confiscate any person's pony.

These two walked carelessly on until they reached a house on the south side of Belgrave Square, which they entered. A couple of letters, just arrived, were still lying on !the hall table; and Lady Silverdale took them up and turned into the dining-room that she might read them. But this spacious and lofty room, with its simple and old-fashioned furniture, was not very well lit in the day-time; and so she walked up to one of the two windows, that she might see to read her letters. She had not opened one of the envelopes when her attention was distracted by the driving up of a hansom; at the same moment she saw a tall, well-built, yellow-bearded man jump out of the cab. Lady Silverdale thought no more of her letters. She heard the bell ring, and swift as lightning she flew to the dining-room door.

"Mitchem," she said, to the man who was about to answer the summons, "where are the young ladies?"

"In the drawing-room, m'lady."

" Show this gentleman into the library."

" Yes, m'lady."

Then she retreated into the dining-room again ; and felt compelled to put aside her Ulster there, and to take off her gloves, for the heat of the place seemed to stifle her. Nevertheless the slender, fair woman, now dressed all in black, looked pale and cold ; and her hands were trembling.

Meanwhile Mr. Frank Cheshunt had been shown into the library, which was immediately behind the dining-room, and there he stood, hat in hand, looking out of the window at a some-what dismal panorama of stables and back-gardens. He was a good-looking man of middle age, not quite so flabby of face as most Englishmen of his type of physique become at forty. More-over, he had just returned from wandering over the wild places of the earth for over a couple of years ; and his ordinarily fair com-plexion was plentifully browned.

He turned as the door opened, and advanced to meet his cousin. She looked a little frightened, and there was less than usual of that sparkling colour in her lips ; but all the same he could not help being struck—even he who knew her so well

—by the singularly youthful and almost girlish grace of this woman. They shook hands rather distantly.

" I am glad to see you are quite well, Mary," said he, affecting a business-like air. " I was afraid you might be down at Woodley. Did you get my letter ? "

" Yes," she said, but she did not look him in the face. " Sit down, Frank. Oh, yes, I got your letter. I suppose you have just arrived ? "

" Last night. I left Venice a day earlier than I had intended."

" You have been a long time away."

" Yes, it seems a long time to me now," said he, taking care not to stare her out of countenance. " I—I got the news in Japan—I—I was very sorry for you, Mary."

Then the pale face flushed ; and she somewhat nervously took up a paper-knife that was lying on the table, and began to bend it. He was sorry he had mentioned that painful circumstance so soon ; he should have waited until the first chill of the meeting had gone off. He noticed her embarrassment, and endeavoured to retrieve his blunder by shifting the subject altogether, and by talking in a light and cheerful strain.

"Do you know," said he, "that during the whole of the four months I was in South America, and more particularly when we were going up the Amazon, I was haunted by an extraordinary delusion—a fancy—a sort of dream. Whenever I lay awake at night, I could not help believing that somehow, when I got up in the morning, I should see Woodley Place right opposite my window; and I should not have been surprised if I had suddenly found myself again fifteen or eighteen years of age. All these later years of my London life seemed to have gone—to have been worth nothing at all; and I had a sort of notion that I ought to go out and ask old Higgins for his gun to shoot the blackbirds in the kitchen-garden. Do you remember the awful damage I once did to the fig-trees?"

She smiled; there was a brighter look on her face now.

"And the time I shot one of Higgins's pigeons, mistaking it for a jay in the twilight?" he said.

"Oh, yes," she answered quickly.

"And the first time your father would let me have a turn at his rabbits—"

" When you lay three hours in a sheep-
trough—"

" And the time you fell into the pond—"

" That was all your fault, Frank."

" And then that dell up by Coney-Bank, where
there were such quantities of blue-bells and primroses in the spring—"

"Yes," she said, with gathering spirit, "and
the dread we had of it after night-fall, because
of the packman—"

"And do you remember that squirrel I gave
you—that bit one of the servants one night at
prayers, and made him squeal out—and your
father getting into such a rage, and declaring
I had set him at the man—"

" I believe you did, Frank."

Her face was radiant. The old days had come
back. They were boy and girl together; making
mischief in the dairy; sitting opposite each other
in the great, damp-smelling family pew; fishing
for sticklebacks in the ponds; gathering violets
by the hedges and in the woods in the sweet,
fresh springtime. Surely this could not be the
woman who was mother of two daughters about
as tall as herself ?

" Ah, well l " said he, with something of a

sigh, " I began to look on all that as having happened only yesterday; and I was sure when the morning came I should get up and look out on the old park, and the ponds, and Woodley Church up on the hill. I—I was glad to forget the intervening years—they had not been very pleasant for me."

She remained silent; but her breath came and went more quickly.

" I wonder," said he, looking at her, " whether one could get quit of a period of one's life by refusing to think of it—whether one could forget—"

He rose, and went forward to her, and took her hand in his.

" Mary," said he, " is it too soon to speak ? "

She rose also, and she did not withdraw her hand until she had answered him.

" I don't know, Frank," she said, in tones so low that he could scarcely hear; but then she raised her beautiful wet eyes to his, and said, with evident emotion, " If I can make up to you, Frank, for all you have suffered—and if you will forgive me for all that is past—I will do what you please."

He kissed her on the forehead, without speaking.

Then a low, booming sound was heard outside in the hall, increasing in volume, followed by a pattering of feet on the stairs.

"You must see the girls, Frank; you will stay and lunch with us, will you not?"

He did stay; but he was rather silent during lunch-time; for he was occupied in studying the faces of the two young ladies and their brother —though he had known them for years—in order to prove to himself that all three were singularly like their mother, and had, in fact, no trace of resemblance to anybody else in their features, voice, or manner.

CHAPTER II.

AN OLD STORY RE-TOLD.

EVERYBODY " in society "—and the much larger number of people outside who take a strange interest in the family affairs of persons of title—knew familiarly the romantic story connected with Mary Cheshunt, subsequently Lady Silverdale. It was a very old story, to be sure, and a very common one ; but it contained those simple elements of romance which have gone to the making up of many thousands of books and plays. Mary Cheshunt was the only daughter of a well-to-do Nottinghamshire squire, whose younger and much poorer brother was a rector just over the borders in Lincolnshire. This clergyman had a son, Frank Cheshunt, who, as a boy, spent a great part of his holidays at Woodley Place, the house of his uncle, and had for his chief companion and playmate his cousin Mary. That was all very well in the days of bird's-nesting and pony-riding ; but it became very different when young Cheshunt, home from Cambridge, betrayed a high appreciation of something else at Woodley Place besides his uncle's hares and pheasants. In fact, the two cousins fell over head and ears in love with each other before they themselves found it out; and it was only when John Cheshunt, consulting with his wife, came to the conclusion that their nephew Frank was too frequent a visitor at the Place, and decided to give him a hint to that effect, that the two young people declared themselves to each other, and swore that nothing on earth should part them. However, John Cheshunt and his wife had come to a contrary resolution. Frank was an exceedingly nice young fellow ; and he promised to make his way in the world ; but all that he could have from his father, the clergyman, was a thoroughly good education, and a pittance of a couple of hundred a year or so. Then the young Lord Silverdale, who had just succeeded to the title, and whose spacious woods and forests adjoined the humbler coverts of Woodley Place, had, in his silent and solemn way, betrayed a considerable regard for his neighbour's ¡daughter, and always accepted invitations to Woodley Place, though it was well known that he never visited, and considered dinner parties an intolerable nuisance. All these things led up to a climax; then there was much weeping and passionate imploring, and secret vows of constancy; after which Mary Cheshunt was cárried off by her parents to Florence, and her cousin did not even hear a word of her for many a day.

Mary Cheshunt was not a heroine. If the course of true love had run smoothly, she would doubtless have married her cousin, and made him a good wife. But this was impossible; she could not think of disobeying her father and making her mother wretched; Silverdale, with all his silent solemnity, and his premature bald-ness, which looked odd in a man of eight-and-twenty, was a highly worthy and respectable young fellow; and it would be nice to have a town house in Belgrave Square. When the Cheshunts, having remained some months in Florence, started for the Nile, Lord Silverdale accompanied them; and the next thing that Frank Cheshunt saw or heard of them was a statement in a morning paper that a marriage had been " arranged " between his rival and his faithless cousin.

Of course, he flew into a series of violent frenzies; at one time vowing to himself that he would go and shoot the man who had stolen his sweetheart's love from him; at another declaring ruthless war with the perjured aristocracies of all countries; at another resolving to write a book that would hold the mirror up to heartless women and cause them to blush—if any shame were left in them—at the picture of their own meanness, and cruelty, and corruption. Happily for himself, he had his living to work for; and these wild schemes were unable to struggle against the immediate pressure of actual facts.

He had come up to London from Cambridge with a fair reputation for ability, and he was busily reading for the Bar—not with a view to practice, but that he might be qualified to accept from the Government one of those appointments which the Cheshunts of Woodley had a fair right to claim as the reward of many years' devotion to the Conservative interests of the country. So he turned with a sick heart to his books again; and tried to forget his false love.

A year or two went by; the newspapers told him that Lady Silverdale was here, there, or elsewhere; but he had never seen her: the newspapers, too, were beginning to talk about him—occasionally and briefly. He had got called to the Bar; but he had suddenly forfeited all his chances of political patronage from the party then in power by joining an informal association of what were at the time known as "Aristocratic Radicals," and becoming one of their most vehement speakers and pamphleteers. Some of those young noblemen and gentlemen had a mild way of toying with revolution over their claret, and spoke of barricades in the same breath with blue china; while having been compelled by the higher criticism to give up revealed religion, they had consoled themselves with a gentle deification of the British workman. But there was no *dilettante* mildness about Frank Cheshunt's professions of faith. When, in the pages of some review, the initials "F. C." were discovered, most readers who busied themselves with politics knew what to expect—keen and trenchant English—a trifle rhetorical, perhaps, with the enthusiasm of youth; a frank insistance on following out theories to their logical conclusion; and an indignant protest against the political apathy of the English people. It was no use laughing at this man; he had to be answered ; and he was strong enough to make people angry. His enemies, on the other hand, were rejoiced to see that he could not get into Parliament, though he tried one or two boroughs where his friends declared he was safe. He had no money ; and the somewhat noisy crowds whom he harangued at public meetings appeared to have no votes. At all events, he cut a poor figure at the poll ; and the scorners had their will of him. " In my distress I called upon the working man,"—this was the substance of their jibes,—" but there was none to answer me."

In the intervals of this busy, eager, active life he had his fits of despairing Wertherism, kept carefully sacred to himself. Those men who met him every day had no idea of the well-spring of sentiment that kept bubbling up within the heart of this hard-hitting, keen-speeched man ; but all the women, of course, knew how he had been jilted, and judged by his conduct in society that he never meant to marry. Sometimes, sitting alone by himself at night, he would go back to the old days, dream for a while, and then seek refuge in Alfred de Musset or Heinrich Heine. Grief seemed more bearable when it was put into

musical words. And if there was a terrible
agony in Heine's picture—

> *Das war ein lustig Hochzeitfest,*
> *Zu Tafel sassen froh die Gäst',*
> *Und wie ich nach dem Brautpaar schaut',*
> *Oh weh! mein Liebchen war die Braut,*

there was some proud remembrance in these lines
of De Musset's—

> *Je me dis seulement, " A cette heure, en ce lieu,*
> *Un jour, je fus aimé, elle était belle.*
> *J'enfouis ce trésor dans mon âme immortelle,*
>   *Et je l'emporte à Dieu ! "*

while sometimes—but very rarely—some wild,
hopeless, passionate wish of his heart startled
even himself—

> *O that 'twere possible,*
> *After long grief and pain,*
> *To find the arms of my true love*
> *Round me once again !*

He never doubted for a moment that Mary
Cheshunt was still Mary Cheshunt—that the
grown woman must have been the perfect fulfil-
ment of all his boyish dreams. She was still to
him the one woman in all the world. There was
no other ; there could be no other. A blue-book

was about as interesting to him as the faces of the women whom he saw.

He met her—by accident. He was at the foot of a steep and narrow staircase, and he was trying to make his way up through a crowd of men and women in order to shake hands with his hostess, and then get off to his club. At length he managed to gain the landing; and there before him—looking at him with rather a frightened, pitiful face—was his cousin. The wrench his heart got then was known to none. She might have been an acquaintance of yester-day to whom he said,—

" Oh, how do you do, Lady Silverdale ? "

He did not offer her his hand ; but she put out hers.

" I am so glad to see you, Frank," said she, with superb composure, but with a wistful en-treaty for kindness in her eyes. " Let me introduce you to my husband—"

" I have met Lord Silverdale before," said Cheshunt, as the silent man with the black hair speckled with white tufts bowed.

She made him promise to call and see them ; and this he did, for he began to grow ashamed of his Wertherism, and thought he could do nothing better than make the friendly acquaintance of the Silverdale family, children included. But it was only an acquaintance, kept up perforce. He knew very little of Lady Silverdale. He could see that she was a fashionable woman, and had ways and manners different from those to which Mary Cheshunt was given ; but she was still to him Mary Cheshunt.

His attention, however, was carried away from these sentimental fancies to more practical matters. There was a man called Alexander Thompson, to whom a kind Providence had given a constitution capable of withstanding the climate of the Gold Coast—a fact which promised well for his comfort anywhere else, whether in this world or the next. Thompson was one of a small handful of merchants, for whose exclusive benefit the British Government maintained one of the most unhealthy settlements on that unhealthy coast—sending out its servants, civil and military, to be buried there, or invalided home with the seeds of fever and dysentery ineradicably implanted in their systems. The place was of no manner of use to us ; the settlement, notwithstanding the exertions of the

Wesleyan missionaries, had most thoroughly demoralized the adjoining tribes; it was hopelessly insolvent, and its chief export to England was sick officials demanding pensions. But it had plenty of exports for other parts of the world; and the handful of merchants waxed fat on their profits.

When Mr. Alexander Thompson returned to England, one might have thought he would be grateful for what the Government had done for him. Most Scotchmen, it is true, are born Radicals, the national constitution not having as yet been mellowed by a few centuries of roast beef and port wine. But then it is as fairly to be supposed that Thompson, having made a large sum of money, would, on returning to England, prefer the respectability of Toryism; or, at the very least, profess himself a reformer until he had gained entrance into the most comfortable club in London, and then have sunk into the gentle Conservatism which is the prevailing political feeling within that institution. Strange to say, Thompson showed himself as fierce an opponent of all governments as any Irishman who has been six months in New York. Nothing but rank Communism would do for him

—theoretical Communism, that is to say; for of course a man who had worked hard for a fortune could not be expected to share it among the poor. He bought for himself a big house in Palace Gardens; he had it luxuriously furnished; and he gave elaborate dinners to those young men—mostly younger sons, it is true—who were vastly discontented with existing institutions. He acquired a pretty taste of his own, too, in the way of luxury. A lady once asked him where he got a certain very beautiful service of dinner glass, as she was anxious to have some of the same; to which he replied that, wishing to have this service unique, he had had the moulds broken. The theory of Communism, one sees, has its limitations in practice.

Now Mr. Thompson betrayed a very special liking for Frank Cheshunt. More than one of the revolutionary Honourables who frequented the house had rather a trick of standing with their back to the fire after dinner and silently staring through a single eye-glass; whereas Mr. Thompson had a particular dislike to being stared at through a single eye-glass. Frank Cheshunt he found to be a plain-spoken, thorough, and altogether earnest fellow; and at last he swore by all the gods that had ever been worshipped on the Gold Coast or elsewhere that he would get Cheshunt into Parliament, if money would do it. We know quite well that money cannot. Mr. Thompson had doubtless formed a commercial view of English public life while supplying the Africans with fierce spirit and sham cotton fabrics. Sure enough, however, Frank Cheshunt got into Parliament.

To sit below the gangway on the Liberal side of the House was at that time to be identified with the pulling down of park-railings and other wicked actions ; and there was a good deal of strong language being used here and there. When Cheshunt by accident stumbled into one or other of these journalistic controversies, he generally managed to give as hard knocks as he got ; but this only proved him to be all the more a dangerous person. It was no matter for wonder, therefore, that Lady Silverdale's eldest daughter, puzzling her small head over stray references in the newspapers, had arrived at the conclusion that her Uncle Frank was a desperate character, who wished to kill the Queen and confiscate everybody's property. A great many folks in society, however—and these mostly of the gentler sex—took a more kindly view of the young man's Radicalism. It was all, according to them, the result of his having been thrown over for wealth and a title; and although they did not blame Lady Silverdale severely for having followed her parents' wishes, they considered his remaining unmarried as rather a touching spectacle—the spectacle of the traditional jilted but faithful lover.

To wind up this hurried sketch of the history of these two people previous to their meeting formerly described, it only remains to be added that two important events happened in Frank Cheshunt's life within the same year. Mr. Thompson died, leaving him a very considerable fortune; and he lost his seat in Parliament. He then took it into his head that he would travel; and it was in Japan that he learned from a newspaper which had been sent him that his old sweetheart had become a widow. He did not go post-haste back to England. He waited until two years of her widowhood had expired; and then, as we have seen, he drove up to her house in Belgrave Square in an ordinary and prosaic hansom.

CHAPTER III.

RÉCHAUFFÉ D'AMOUR.

VERY speedily all the world got to know, or to guess, that Lady Silverdale was about to marry her cousin—her sweetheart of former days ; and it was considered that now their romantic story had reached its proper end. But however little romanticism remained in the heart of Frank Cheshunt—who was now a tall, robust, yellow-bearded Englishman of eight and thirty years of age, who had seen a good deal of the world and had his share of interest in public life—he did not at all look at the matter in that light. He determined that, so far as he was able, the long interval which had separated him from his love of early days should be a blank. They should both ignore that hapless time and all its associations. They were to start a new life together, and forget the past. He was ready even to give up England for her sake, if she for his sake would do as much ; and then they might go away to some distant home, by the side of a blue lake, and there, content with each other's society, learn to think no more of the time during which they had been separated than if it had been a dream. It is perhaps needless to point out that these vague aspirations were but the incipient signs of retrospective jealousy— one of the most perilous of the passions.

To his surprise and regret he found that his beautiful sweetheart was far less imaginative and romantic than himself. She did not at all care about being married at once and leaving England, just as the London season was about to begin. But she did not precisely tell him that she preferred another London season to the early enjoyment of his society by the side of that far blue lake. She represented that any undue haste on their part would shock their friends. Then there was a great deal to be done about sending Maudey and her sister to a school at Dresden. Finally, it was necessary to guard against any disrespect to the dead—and here, of course, Frank Cheshunt at once, and in awkward silence, gave in. After all, he loved his cousin ; and he was sure that her tender heart would tell her what was right.

But he grew—during these few months of waiting—to hate the circle of friends and acquaintances in which she moved. They conspired, with great kindness, to bring these two together; but then they continually talked of matters relating to that long period which he had resolved to ignore; appearing to be far better acquainted with Lady Silverdale than himself. They led his cousin, too, into all sorts of fashionable foibles; and dragged her about; and induced her to talk frivolity just like themselves. If he had not known Mary Cheshunt, he would have said that Lady Silverdale was an ordinary, empty-headed woman of fashion, who was exceedingly pretty, and dressed well when her dress did not happen to be a trifle too pronounced. He was sure, indeed, that this was not the proper atmosphere for his beautiful bride-elect. Mary Cheshunt had never been a popinjay. When should he be able to carry her off to those calm and peaceful solitudes where the heart could speak freely without risk of being ashamed?

He was all the more ready to make this sacrifice on his own side—if it could be considered a sacrifice—from the fact that he had but recently returned from two years' residence abroad ; and he had not had time to resume much interest in English public affairs. In fact, there was little doing at the time. The leader of one political party had gone off in high dudgeon to fell trees and write for magazines, leaving his followers somewhat bewildered ; the leader of the other party, finding his opponents without a policy, and himself therefore unable to appropriate it, was quite content to wait. Certain outsiders, it is true, were anxious to put into the pauperized peasant's hand something he could give in exchange for the blankets, port wine, and Christmas puddings received from the squire's wife and the parson—that *quid pro quo* being a vote ; and the squire and the parson were not much alarmed by this proposal, for they knew very well how they could use that vote against a party which was supposed to be directing a baleful eye on the National Church. Neither the lowering of the County Franchise, however, nor Disestablishment was near enough to awaken much interest ; and Frank Cheshunt found his afternoons at the Reform Club chiefly taken up with playing whist. He could have left England at that time with little regret.

As it was, he consoled himself with the hope that when once he had got his sweetheart clear away from all old associations, he would make her life so happy that she would be well-disposed to remain wherever he pleased ; and in the meantime a great deal had to be done to make this plan possible. Happily, Lady Silverdale had already, before seeing him, resolved to send her two daughters to Dresden ; but it required an infinite amount of argument and persuasion to convince her that the young Lord Silverdale ought to be sent to live with Frank Cheshunt's father, the old clergyman having kindly under-taken to coach the boy for Eton. At last she did consent ; and another obstacle was then re-moved. But what did she mean by never speaking of the neighbourhood in which they were to live when they returned from their wedding-tour ? Did she suppose for a moment that he, Frank Cheshunt, was coming back to live in that house in Belgrave Square, or even at Woodley Manor ? His face burned at the very thought of it. But whatever she may have thought—or forgotten—he was happily absolved from the necessity of taking and furnishing a house, which would have been a desperate encumbrance in the event of his persuading her to remain with him at Ouchy.

At length the time drew near when they were to be married; and it was necessary to make arrangements for their wedding trip. It was at this point they had their first quarrel—or something approaching a quarrel—for Lady Silverdale insisted on taking her maid, an old servant of the Silverdale family, with her. Cheshunt, with great gentleness and affection, remonstrated; then, finding that she persisted, grew indignantly angry.

"How could I travel without her, Frank?" her ladyship pleaded. "I have never travelled without her—"

"Gracious heavens!" he said, "how do other women travel without a maid, then?"

"I should lose all my things—"

"Cannot I look after your luggage?"

"She knows everything, and she has been everywhere with us—"

"Not with us," said he, with bitter sarcasm; driven to speak of a subject which he ordinarily avoided as if it were poison. "You forget, Mary. I have not the pleasure of the woman's acquaintance. I should consider her a nuisance

—an impertinent intrusion—why, on a man's wedding trip, to be haunted by some old fool of a woman—"

Lady Silverdale rose.

"I am sorry to hear you use such language, Frank. Holmes is a most respectable person; and she has always been treated with the greatest consideration by my husband's family."

He was rather a hot-tempered man.

"When I asked you to marry me, Mary," said he, "I did not undertake to marry your late husband's family, and his man-servants, and his maid-servants, and the confounded number of asses within his gates. So you had better consider the matter."

He took his leave; and she, cold, and silent, and proud, merely bowed to him as he went out. He went up to the club, read an evening paper, yet saw nothing on the page before him; played a rubber at whist, and made two revokes, which called down on his head a fair amount of bad language. Then he dressed, and dined by himself—choosing a small table so that no one should be able to sit down with him. He was to have met Lady Silverdale at a party that evening; and he was resolved not to go near the place ; but if he was not going, why had he taken the trouble to dress ?

Lovers of eight and thirty and five and thirty have happily more common sense than younger persons ; and this quarrel was easily made up. Lady Silverdale was pacified by a most ample apology for his unjustifiable rudeness ; and she, on the other hand, agreed to give up the invaluable Holmes. Yet she could not understand why her cousin had betrayed such a dislike to Holmes. Nor could she understand why, when she had to go down to Woodley Manor, he would not come and see her, though his own father was coming over to carry off the youthful heir. The plain fact was that she did not perceive how anxious he was to consider that long period of separation as never having existed ; while she was continually harping on what she did this year or the other year, and what Lord Silverdale had said on this or the other occasion. But Frank Cheshunt forgave much to his beautiful cousin ; knowing that he would soon have ample time to explain to her all his views about their coming life together, when perhaps she, too, would resolve to forget.

D

CHAPTER IV.

REVELATIONS.

" O that 'twere possible,
After long grief and pain ;
To find the arms of my true love
Round me once again ! "

THIS had been the secret, yearning cry of
Frank Cheshunt, as it has been the cry of
thousands on thousands of other people, who,
even in married life sometimes, have been visited
by moments of sentimental regret, when they
believed that their life might have been other
than it is. Very well, then. He had his wish.
When everybody heard of Lady Silverdale and
her old lover having gone off on their wedding
trip, it was universally conceded that poetic
justice had been awarded, and the romance
happily and fitly come to an end.

He took her down to Dover—to a hotel where
the Mumm's " extra dry " is very good, and the
drainage very bad. Anxious as he was to leave
England and all its associations behind, he never-

theless gladly consented to stay in Dover for two or three days, for the sea was not quite a mill-pond, and Lady Silverdale had a horror of a rough passage. When he pointed out to her that there was not a white line on the sea, and not a breath of wind anywhere, and yet found her unwilling to cross, he generously yielded to her timid fears. But when he found that, by waiting, she had managed to receive a budget of letters from Woodley Manor, and was disposed to seek his advice about certain propositions of her land-steward, he put on his hat and walked out, and for about three-quarters of an hour smoked a cigar on the pier.

"I hope," said he, when he returned, "that you don't mean to have letters dogging your footsteps all over the Continent?"

"My dear Frank," said she, looking up in perfect innocence, "we are not going into banishment, are we?"

But after all he had to be considerate towards this beautiful bride of his, if she should not understand all his imaginative purposes and wishes all at once. And now he found her ready to cross the Channel at any moment. That night the water was smooth as glass; there was scarcely a ripple in the harbour to break the reflection of the stars. They got their things on board; and remained on deck during the whole of the passage. When they reached Calais pier, he had of course all the bother of looking after rugs and hand-bags, and so forth, of which she had a considerable stock; and when they had got up and into Calais station, he proposed they should have a basin of soup, or some such thing, before getting to sleep in the carriage that was to take them on to Brussels. But all her anxiety was to send a telegram to Maudey, at Dresden, announcing the safe voyage across the Channel. He did not see the fun of blundering about this gloomy station in the middle of the night.

"You telegraphed to her yesterday," said he, rather impatiently, "what on earth is the good of telegraphing now?"

"I am sure the dear child will be so anxious until she knows I am safely over."

"I hope the dear child is in bed," said he.

"She would get the telegram the first thing in the morning," his wife responded, and then she added regretfully, "If Holmes had been with us, I could have sent her at once—she was very clever at doing these little things for me."

"Shall I put the telegram in French or English?" said he abruptly; and then he stalked off to send that message to the "Honble. Maud Calesthorpe, Pension Grimm, Nudelsuppe-strasse, No. 49, Dresden."

They spent a day in Brussels, or rather in the Rue Montagne de la Cour, for Lady Silverdale greatly admired the shops, particularly the lace shops, in that thoroughfare; and she said she liked to hear her own tongue spoken by the people about her who were staring in at the windows. He bought some trifles for her; she bought some presents for Maudey, Ernestine, and Harry.

Now on his recent return from distant lands Cheshunt had come home by way of the Rhine; and at Cologne had stumbled across a hotel which has a very pretty balcony, or "Belvedere," right at the top of it, from which one has a commanding view of the Rhine, and of the distant country around the Drachenfels. At that time he imagined to himself, if only his old sweetheart would now consent to marry him, the pleasure he would have in leading her up to this lofty balcony, and showing her the broad and flowing river and the distant ramparts that

guard the entrance to the great valley of romance.
But when they got to Cologne, he found that
she knew the hotel very well; and did not think
it worth while to undertake the fatigue of climb-
ing to the Belvedere; and was mostly curious
to know how far Dresden was from Cologne. In
fact, she had a familiar acquaintance with the
Rhine. She had spent a month at Konigswinter,
when Maudey was recovering from the measles.
Did he know that Maudey's sketches of Roland-
seck and its neighbourhood had been shown to
no less a person than Mr. Ruskin, who had not
at all condemned them. Had he ever heard
Maudey sing "The Lorelei"? In his secret
heart Lady Silverdale's husband coupled the
name of Maudey with an expletive which was
quite uncalled-for, and indeed so improper that
it cannot be put down here.

However, when they got to Geneva, and he
found she had never been there before, nor yet
to Chamounix, things looked better; and now
he felt they were really setting out on their
wedding tour, leaving the world behind them.
At eight o'clock on a beautiful bright summer
morning, they got into the large and open
carriage which had been ordered over-night.

The scarlet-coated driver cracked his long whip; the four horses, ornamented with foxes' tails and pheasant's feathers, started off at a rattling pace, with all their bells jingling; they crossed the bridge that spans the blue and rushing waters of the Rhone; they took a last look at the broad and still bosom of the lake; and then away they went—all by themselves—towards the deep and beautiful valley lying under the white snows of Mont Blanc.

"At last," said he, "Mary, we have got clear away from England; and I don't care whether I ever see it again."

"I think you would soon tire of perpetual holidays, Frank," said she, with a smile; but she put her hand into his, and he felt contented and happy.

Suddenly she looked round at the rugs and bags with which the interior of the open carriage was filled.

"Where is that batch of newspapers that came yesterday?" she asked.

"Newspapers?" said he, lightly. "What do we want with newspapers? I left them."

"Indeed, Frank, you should have brought them on; you ought to be ready to take your own part in public affairs when we go back; for a man gets so much more consideration shown him when he is in Parliament; and of course the Liberals will get in again; and they might give you some office; and then you know how important it would be for the girls, by and by, to go to the official receptions and such things—"

"My dear Mary," said he, with some firmness, "we will leave all that alone for the present. I think we ourselves are entitled to some little consideration; and if it suited us not to return to England for some time—for an indefinite period—politics would get on very well without us; and so I am sure would those charming young ladies about whom you feel so anxious." She detected no sarcasm in his tone. She said innocently,—

"They are really such good girls; you will love them more the more you see of them; and you know you will have to be a father to the poor things, Frank. Fancy their being away all by themselves in that strange town—"

"I suppose this must be Chesne," said he rudely.

Every one who drives from Geneva to Chamounix ought to stop at the small village of

St. Martin, where, while lunch is being got ready, he may walk down to the bridge over the river, from which the first impressive view of Mont Blanc is to be obtained. Frank Cheshunt and his bride did so ; and as they leaned on the stone parapet, over the chalky-green and rushing waters, they found before them the great white shoulders of Mont Blanc standing far, and high, and clear in a cloudless blue sky. It was a spectacle that called for silence.

"It is very pretty," said Lady Silverdale. "Really, the white and the blue are exactly like—"

"Like one of Maudey's drawings?" said he, fiercely. "Is it literally impossible for you to look at any given object, or to pass a single moment in the society of any being, without continually harping on Maudey and Ernestine, and Ernestine and Maudey?"

She did not answer him. She turned her head away, and tears began to run down her cheeks. He knew he had been a brute.

"Come, Mary," said he, and he took hold of her arm, "you must forgive me. I am very sorry. I did not mean to hurt you."

For the rest of that day she maintained a

strict silence as regarded Maudey and Ernestine
—an enforced silence that was perhaps more
irritating than free speech. It raised a certain
barrier between them. When they reached their
hotel at Chamounix, about six o'clock in the
evening, she went up to her room, saying that
she had a headache and would lie down. She
failed to appear at dinner; preferring a cup of
tea and a bit of dry toast. So he dined at the
table-d'hôte without her ; made the acquaintance
of nobody ; and after dinner, in the cool, clear
evening, went off for a long leisurely walk along
the road leading through the valley, that he
might smoke his cigar in peace. He was not
thinking now of Maudey, nor yet of Ernestine,
nor yet of his old fair love of former days ; but
of an interview which he had had with Lord
Hartington about a week before he had started.
He had also had a talk with Mr. Adam. Frank
Cheshunt was no longer the fierce irreconcilable
he had been in his hot youth. In his wander-
ings abroad he had come to doubt the saving
virtues of more than one party Shibboleth. But
he still professed himself a Liberal ; and he had
paid his subscription to the Devonshire as his
humble tribute to the reconstruction of his party.

He was thinking at this moment that, after all, it was not good for a man to be idle. And if the prospect of a General Election were remote, vacancies were still occurring by death and promotion to the Lords, in which case it was always better for a man who wanted to slip quietly into a seat to be on the spot. No one knew how his country might suffer by his absence.

CHAPTER V

"THE PITY OF IT, IAGO."

THEY remained about ten days or a fortnight at Chamounix, making all the orthodox excursions, except the Jardin, which Lady Silverdale was afraid to attempt. She had forgotten or forgiven that little episode at St. Martin, and was quite as much disposed as ever to chat cheerfully about her dear girls. When she climbed up to the Glacier des Bossons she brought away souvenirs for them; when she got to Montanvert she gathered ferns for them ; when she was carefully handed over the rounded and slippery blocks of the Mer de Glace she shudderingly looked at the deep blue crevices on either hand, and declared that she would never allow her children to cross that terrible place—a decision she adhered to all the more when she had clambered down the Mauvais Pas, clinging to the iron rope, and not daring to turn her eyes for a moment towards the sheer precipice beneath her feet.

And Frank Cheshunt, being a good-natured, reasonable fellow, argued with himself, and tried to persuade himself that it was but natural for his wife to be continually thinking about Maudey. Do not all women who have children bore their relatives 'and friends by persistent talking about these infant prodigies? And here was a mother taken away from her children for the first time. If the truth were told—and the object of this story is to tell the truth—it was not alone her constant talking about her children that somewhat painfully disappointed Lady Silverdale's husband. He found that their tastes were very different, and that she was not a little opinionated. He was shocked to find, for example, that she greatly admired a species of novel which he particularly detested—and here they might have been content to differ; but when he proceeded to show that these descriptions of life and manners were only fit for the scullery and the stable, he was met by an exhibition of will and temper that pretty plainly warned him off attempting to convert his wife to his views about literature. She was not a strong woman in any way. Her natural detestation of one whom she considered to be the perjured and treacherous assassin of innocent women and children, and of an event which she considered to be the blackest crime in modern history, melted away before the solvent influence of an invitation to dine at St. Cloud, and she acquired a thoroughly *bourgeois* delight in the spangle-glitter of Paris. She was rather dense, too, as regarded a joke, and consequently very apt to take offence at perfectly good-natured raillery. The mere mention of certain subjects seemed to freeze her into an icicle ; she knew that her husband was going to say something that would wound her feelings. Bishops, for instance ; why is it that gentlemen who profess Liberal opinions should be so fond of making fun of bishops, who are a most respectable class of persons when they are rightly understood ? Now the moment that Frank Cheshunt began to talk about a bishop, his wife froze. He was nearly proposing a compromise on this matter—offering to cut out the whole bench from his conversation, if she would consent to cut out Maudey from hers. But he refrained from making the suggestion, for she would most certainly have construed it into an attack on the Established Church.

At this point of the narrative the writer would like to put in a disclaimer. The reader may, as his temperament suggests, object to this story as impertinently flippant, or as too painfully miserable, or as fiendishly malicious. But he must not regard it as written with a purpose. It would be a mistake to suppose that if every man who now, in the quiet jog-trot of married life, thinks of the early love of his youth, and perhaps deplores the imagined happiness that then vanished out of his grasp—it would be a mistake to suppose that every such man, had he married his early love, would have found her out to be an unmistakable ass. We are now dealing only with Frank Cheshunt and Lady Silverdale, and their story, which every one assures you is so romantic. Painful as the task may be, it becomes necessary to tell the simple truth about that romance.

The first time they went up to Montanvert they saw a wonderful sight. Up to that period the weather had been too fine, and they had grown tired of looking up at the great white shoulder of Mont Blanc standing clear against the blue sky. But on this occasion great moving and ragged masses of fog lay over the Mer de

Glace, entirely shutting off the mountains beyond; and when they and the guide proceeded to descend from Montanvert to cross the glacier, they could see nothing at all in front of them. Suddenly, however, Cheshunt uttered an exclamation. His eye had somehow been attracted upward, and there, apparently overhead, above the long and shifting swathes of fog, and seeming to belong to another world, rose far away into the unimaginable distance long glittering spires and pinnacles of rock, gleaming in a sunshine that came from a sky which they could not see. It was their first revelation of the awful height of this mountain-land, and it had come upon them in the form of a vision; for these scarred and snow-spreckled Aiguilles, that shone away up there in the intense and distant blue, seemed to be glittering, beautiful phantoms that had sprung upwards to this amazing altitude from the witch's cauldron of whirling and changing fog. Cheshunt had seen many sights in his time, but even he was overawed by the incomparable majesty and splendour of this weird thing, and for a second or two he could not speak. His wife came to his relief.

"Oh, Frank, isn't it beautiful?" she said, in simple faith. "I never saw anything like that before. It reminds one of that beautiful picture of heaven—you remember."

"Oh, yes," he said quickly, "Martin's. It is quite like that. Shall I carry your alpenstock for you until we get down to the ice?"

She got very tired of Chamounix before they left. She did not at all like this rough work of jolting about on mules; it sadly disarranged her toilette. Then they had not met a single acquaintance, though they tried the *tables-d'hôte* of the associated hotels in succession. She used to glance over *Galignani* after dinner, and read out to her husband the names of her friends who, as she saw, were in Paris.

At last they set out from Chamounix—Lady Silverdale mounted on a patient mule, her husband walking by her side, and an attendant bringing up a spare mule in the rear. They made a picturesque group enough, and it was a day fit to be remembered specially even in a wedding-tour. He was a good specimen of the stalwart, manly Englishman; her beautiful refined face had got some touch of colour in it from the cool fresh winds; and they were slowly

E

ascending the pass of the Tête Noire, which is the grandest pass in Europe, with the sunlight shining on the wonderful snow-peaks all around them. They ought to have been content.

Somehow Frank Cheshunt was not quite so hopeful as he had been about that project of his, which was now about to be tried. He had spoken to his wife, timidly and tentatively, about the beauties of the Lake of Geneva. He had described the clear blue waters, the fair skies, the panorama of mountains, the white walls of the Castle of Chillon reflected in the crystal deeps. He had described, too, a spacious villa, set amid gardens, with quaint eaves and green casements; its gleaming white front variegated here and there by trellis-work; its garden walls a mass of crimson with Virginia Creepers; its cool summer-house by the side of the lake. She said it was very nice, but she did not add that she would care to live all her life at Ouchy.

It was well on towards evening when they drew near the Martigny; and as they went down the mountain-side, passing through the twilight of the dense forests, she looked like some princess of Romance attended by her faithful squire on foot. She was cheerful, too, with

a new cheerfulness that surprised him after all
the fatigues of the day. The fact was, she had
inquired of the mule-driver, and learned that
they should pass the post-office in going into
Martigny, and there she expected to get a whole
batch of letters from Dresden, Lincolnshire,
Nottinghamshire, and London.

They stopped in passing, and her husband very
willingly went into the post-office. It was but
natural she should want to have her letters; she
had received none for two or three days. When
he came out, however, and said that there was
not even one for her, she grew terribly alarmed.
Something dreadful must have happened. They
had acted in concert to keep back the news. He
must telegraph at once to Maudcy, to his uncle,
to everybody.

"Nonsense," said he; "can't you wait till the
morning? There is a post in at ten."

She was hurt by his cruel indifference; but
she consented to wait. The whole evening she
was silent and *distraite :* he could scarcely get a
word out of her. Next morning she was at the
post-office by half-past nine, just to see if the
mails might not be in sooner than usual. They
were later than usual. When they did arrive,

she almost refused to believe the postmaster that there was not a single letter for her.

She walked quickly back to the hotel; her husband was standing in the archway, smoking a cigar. She went past him without speaking, and he noticed something peculiar about her expression.

"Hallo, Mary, where are you going?" said he.

She turned for a moment; there was a sparkle of anger in her eyes, in the midst of all her dread.

"I must get money to telegraph for myself, I suppose," she said, "since you won't. There is not a single letter. I know something has happened."

"Better wait till two," said he; "there is another post in from England then."

She did not answer. She went up and got her purse, and then walked off to the post-office, where she bothered the poor postmaster for half an hour with her applications and inquiries. Ultimately, as it turned out, there was not the least occasion for all this worry. She received a telegram from Maudey saying that all was well, but she had neglected to write. She received a

telegram from London saying all was well, but
that the last batch of letters had been forwarded
by mistake to Chamounix instead of Martigny.

"Very well," said her husband ; " now we can
go on to Ouchy. We will send a message to
Chamounix to forward letters there."

But she would not hear of that. She would
remain in Martigny until the letters arrived.
She could not go on without her letters from
London.

At this point his patience broke down.

" I wish to Heaven," he said savagely—but he
really did not intend her to hear, " that you had
never left London ! "

" Do you wish," said she, turning round and
becoming rather pale, " do you wish, Frank, that
you had never married me ? "

He dared not quite say that, when they were
not much more than a month married ; but he
said, with extreme bitterness,—

" And what then ? Would it concern you ?
You seem to consider your marriage as but a
very trifling accident—of somewhat less impor-
tance than Maudey's toothache, or the building
of the new stables at Woodley Manor."

" I don't quite understand you, Frank," she

said calmly : she had a vague notion that she
was being insulted, or at least injured ; but
she did not exactly know which phrase to com-
plain of.

Once more, however, peace was patched up
between them, Cheshunt spending the best part
of a day and a half in walking up and down the
main street of Martigny, smoking cigars, while
they waited for the precious letters. That batch
of correspondence having at length arrived, they
started for Ouchy ; but now his fond fancy about
beginning a new life there with his sweetheart of
old was distinctly moribund.

It was a beautiful clear forenoon when they
stood on the small wooden pier—I really forget the name of the village—waiting for the
steamer. The skies were blue, the waters were
blue, a soft sunlight lay along the smiling green
shores. Frank Cheshunt was looking rather
blankly out on the smooth, beautiful lake.

"How long do we stay at Ouchy ? " said his
wife ; and somehow the voice that startled him
from his reverie sounded business-like and
harsh.

"I had a fancy," said he, with a smile, " that
we might remain there a long time—if you had

been less occupied with England, Mary. I had some vague wish to take a house there—"

"Oh, I am so glad you no longer think of that," she said quite cheerfully. "Ouchy, of all places in the world! We should not know a soul there; and as for amusements! Now, it is quite remarkable the number of people we know who happen to be in Paris at present. Don't you think we had better get back to Paris as soon as possible, Frank dear?"

"Yes," said he, speaking with measured indifference; "I think we ought at once to make for Paris. And then, as you will be with plenty of friends there, you will not mind my running over to London for a few days. The fact is, —— asked me to let him have that article by the 1st of November, and I must have an afternoon or two in the library at the Reform."

"Well," she said, smiling, "people may think it odd if you return to London by yourself from your wedding trip. But it is only for a day or two?"

"Oh, only for a day or two," said he; the steamer was coming in at the moment, and he was busy about the rugs.

It was on that pier that Frank Cheshunt's

illusory project, based on the assumption that
Lady Silverdale would necessarily prove to be
all that his boyish dreams had imagined Mary
Cheshunt to be, dropped stone-dead ; and as he
was a practical, sensible sort of man, he resolved
to think no more about it. He took his wife to
Paris, and left her in good hands, while he ran
over to London for materials for his magazine
article. The last that I heard of Lady Silverdale
and her husband was that she was temporarily
staying in Dresden, to the great delight of herself and Maudey and Ernestine ; that he was
waging a spirited but hopeless fight in a North
of Scotland borough which had just become
vacant ; and that both he and she were quite—
well, quite comfortable.

So far the story in its plain truth : this may
be added, perhaps, as a guess—that if Frank
Cheshunt should now and again—by some such
accident as happens to many—see a beautiful,
tender face in his dreams—a face familiar, yet
strangely unfamiliar, to him—the face of a
woman whom he has loved, and if his heart
should grow sick with the pain of seeing her
turn away from him ; and if he should follow
with a pitiful agony the receding form wringing

its hands with grief, and withdrawing from him at last the beautiful, bedimmed, never-to-be-forgotten eyes, you may be sure that the face and the figure he beholds with mingled yearning and anguish in these phantom halls of sleep are those not of Lady Silverdale, his wife, but of Mary Cheshunt, his cousin, and his early love.

THE PUPIL OF AURELIUS.

THE PUPIL OF AURELIUS.

CHAPTER I.

A BLOW FACED.

ON a Sunday morning in the early part of November 1878 a stranger arrived at Euston Square, and passed from the gloom of the station into the brighter air of the London streets, there pausing for a second or two to look around him. He was a man of about fifty, short, thin, wiry, square-shouldered; his features firm even to sternness, and hardened by exposure to wind and weather; his hair gray; his beard also gray and clipped short. The harshness of his face, however, was in a measure tempered by the look of his eyes; these were calm and contemplative, perhaps even with a shade of melancholy in them. For the rest, he was well and warmly clad in home-spun cloth; and he carried with

him a small hand-bag, which appeared to be his
only luggage.

He hesitated only for a moment. As he
turned off to the left he met two labourers
coming along.

" This is the way to London Bridge, is it
not ? " he asked, slowly, and with a strong
northern accent.

" Yes, sir," said one of them ; and then, as he
looked after the departing stranger, he took the
pipe from his mouth and grinned, and said to
his companion :

" Scottie means to walk it."

The new-comer's next encounter was less satis-
factory. A drunken-faced woman jumped up
from a door-step and begged for alms. He had
not seen her. Instinctively his hand went to
his pocket. Then he glanced at her.

" No ! " he said, with unnecessary severity,
and passed on.

But instantly the woman was transformed
into a cursing and swearing virago. She followed him, making the little thoroughfare
resound with her shrill abuse. Most people
would, in such circumstances, have looked out
for a policeman, or tried to get away somewhere,

but this man turned round and stood still and regarded the woman. There was neither anger nor surprise nor scorn in his look, but a calm observation. He listened to her foul language, as if wishing to understand it; and he regarded the bloated face and bleared eyes. The woman was not prepared for this examination. With another parting volley she slunk off. Then the new-comer continued on his way, saying only to himself:

"It is strange. I do not think that God could have meant any of His creatures to be like that."

Now let us see what manner of man this was who was passing into the larger space and wan sunlight of Euston Road, making for London Bridge, with but little hurry, and always with his eyes [regarding the withered trees, or the closed shops, or the early omnibuses with an observation that had no curiosity in it, rather as if these were mere passing phenomena that left no permanent impression on a mind too busily occupied with its own speculations.

His name was John Douglas. His father had been a small shipowner in Greenock, and, dying, had left this, his eldest son, a fortune of about

£10,000. John Douglas, after patient judgment of the matter, arrived at the conclusion that it was far from just and fitting that he should have the exclusive use of this money, so he lent £7000, or thereabouts, to his two younger brothers, who forthwith took it, and, unhappily, themselves also, to the bottom of the sea, in a vessel which, recklessly, they had not insured. Thereupon John Douglas, having still over £3000, invested it in what was then considered a safe concern, and finding his wants very few and very simple, repaired to the Renfrewshire coast, and found there a small cottage overlooking the Firth of Clyde and the sea, where he could live cheaply and comfortably. And he did live there very comfortably and contentedly, though not quite to the satisfaction of his neighbours, who resented the intrusion amongst them of a man who minded his own business, who would not listen to any tittle-tattle, who was absolutely indifferent as to what opinion, good or ill, they might have of him, and who took long and solitary walks among the hills on Sundays as on other days.

It ought to be said here at the outset that this man's character is not set up as in any way an exemplar. If mankind at large were so many John Douglases the world would not get on at all. We should have no iron bridges built, or Atlantic cables laid, or financial companies started, and we certainly should not have any mankilling machines a million or half-a-million strong ; whereas every well-conducted person knows that such things are now-a-days absolutely necessary. The truth is, that John Douglas, or Captain Douglas, as the neighbours called him with a kind of grudging respect, was a skulker from the battle of humanity. What he wanted was a beach of white sand, a hot day, a blue sea, a book, a pipe, and the absence of his fellow-creatures. He was kind to such people as he was forced to meet ; and he was a favourite amongst the children in that part, for he bought them toys and sweetmeats when he went to Greenock ; but he preferred the society of his books to that of his neighbours, and he was impatient of idle talk. Indeed, what was the use of their conversing with a man who was far more interested in the first blossoming of the furze in spring than in a Cabinet crisis, and who would go away and search for birds' nests in the woods, for the mere pleasure of looking at them,

F

when the whole civilised world, from the Cloch
Lighthouse all the way to Largs, was convulsed
with the news that a minister in a parish adjacent
had been heard to say something disrespectful
about Calvin ?

The three books, one or other of which John
Douglas usually carried with him on his rambles
by sea-shore or through some country lanes,
were the New Testament, Marcus Aurelius, and
Tannahill's Poems ; but perhaps it was the wise
Emperor with whom he most closely communed
as the waves rippled along the sand, and the
shifting lights crossed the clear blue of the
Arran hills. He had so entered into the spirit
of that proud and patient stoicism, that he considered himself proof against anything that
might happen to him in life or in death. It was
a voice from far away, it is true—muffled, as if
from the tomb ; but it was human, sympathetic,
kindly in the main.

"Every moment think steadily as a Roman
and a man to do what thou hast in hand with
perfect and simple dignity, and feeling of affection, and freedom, and justice ; and to give thyself relief from all other thoughts. And thou
wilt give thyself relief, if thou doest every act

of thy life as if it were the last, laying aside all carelessness and passionate aversion from the commands of reason, and all hypocrisy, and self-love, and discontent with the portion which has been given to thee. Thou seest how few the things are, the which if a man lays hold of, he is able to live a life which flows in quiet, and is like the existence of the gods; for the gods, on their part, will require nothing more from him who observes these things."

And again :

" If thou workest at that which is before thee, following right reason seriously, vigorously, calmly, without allowing anything else to distract thee, but keeping thy divine part pure, as if thou shouldst be bound to give it back immediately; if thou holdest to this, expecting nothing, fearing nothing, but satisfied with thy present activity according to nature, and with heroic truth in every word and sound which thou utterest, thou wilt live happy. And there is no man who is able to prevent this."

Or if one should not find any great work in the world to tackle ?—

" Always bear this in mind, that very little

indeed is necessary for living a happy life. And because thou hast despaired of becoming a dialectician, and skilled in the knowledge of nature, do not for this reason renounce the hope of being both free and modest and social and obedient to God."

Or has one been injured?—

" The best way of avenging thyself is not to become like the wrongdoer."

Why should one desire praise or fear blame ?—

" Which of these things is beautiful because it is praised, or spoiled by being blamed? Is such a thing as an emerald made worse than it was if it is not praised? or gold, ivory, purple, a lyre, a little knife, a flower, a shrub ? "

John Douglas knew nothing of the opinion in which he was held by his neighbours ; and, if he had known, he would not have heeded one jot.

Now it was in the waning of the year, when the great fuchsia-tree covering the front of Brae-side Cottage had dropped all its dark-red bells, and when the rowan-trees along the road were yellowing, though masses of the scarlet berries still remained to delight the eye, that the news of the breaking of the City of Glasgow Bank came to these parts. There were those who knew that the residue of Captain Douglas's small fortune was invested in that flourishing concern, which had been paying dividends of 10 and 11 per cent. ; and they also suspected that he would know nothing of the terrible crash, for he seldom read newspapers. But not one of them would go and take the bad news to him. If he had not been a very sociable man, it was not through pride. He had done many generous actions. The children were fond of him. They waited for himself to find out the misfortune that had overtaken him.

Douglas's first intimation was contained in a letter sent him by a solicitor in Greenock. The vague reference to what had happened he did not understand at first ; but he called his old housekeeper and bade her to bring him the newspapers of the last few days ; and then he sat down, quietly and composedly, and read the story of his ruin.

First came the rumours about a certain bank. Then the definite statement that the City of Glasgow Bank had suspended payment. Then guesses at the deficit, beginning with £3,000,000, along with indignant comments about the manner in which the business of the bank had been conducted, and commiseration for the shareholders, the large majority of whom, it was anticipated, would have to surrender every farthing of which they were possessed.

Douglas read on and read through; and was neither shocked nor bewildered. He even remembered something about an official communication which he had opened a day or two before, and hastily dropped in order to fling a book at a strange cat that had come into the garden, and was cowering in wait for a chaffinch. He scarcely knew enough of business to understand who the creditors were; but he could perceive that if they had even £2,000,000 owing to them, the first calls would far more than sweep away his little property and leave him a beggar. Very well. He looked at the newspapers again; there was nothing in these crumpled sheets that could hurt him. A branch of a tree blown down by the wind on the top of his head could hurt him; or a chimney-pot falling from a roof; or a horse lifting its leg and kicking him; but a newspaper report he could thrust into the fire. He looked out of the window; the broad waters of the Firth were all ruffled into a dark blue by the morning breeze, and the sunlight shone along the yellow shores of Innellan; and far in the south Arran's jagged peaks were a clear blue among the silvery clouds: these things could not be altered by anything happening in Glasgow. He looked at his hands; there were ten fingers there that had not done much work in the world; surely it was time they should try? And surely they could win for him bread and milk, or at the worst bread and water? In the meantime the thought of the cat had recalled to him that he had not as yet scattered crumbs for the birds that morning. That was the first thing to be done; and so he went and did it.

There can be no doubt that this contemptuous indifference was largely the result of the teachings of Marcus Aurelius, which this solitary man had drunk in until they seemed to have got absorbed into his very blood. But there was something more; there was a vein of personal pride of a very distinct kind. He would not admit to himself that any number of bank-directors in Glasgow or elsewhere had the power to harm him. Moreover, when, after

waiting a considerable time to see how things
would go, he went to Greenock to consult the
solicitor who had written to him, and to whom
he was known, this stubborn pride and
independence came out more strongly than
ever.

"The question is," said he in his slow, em-
phatic way, "do I owe the money, or do I not
owe the money ? "

"No doubt of it, Captain Douglas," the other
remonstrated ; "you are morally as well as
legally bound. But the liquidators are human
beings ; they do not wish to press for the utter-
most farthing ; and well they know that this
first call of £500 on every £100 of stock will
ruin many and many a poor creature, and turn
him or her out into the world. There is even a
talk of a Relief Fund ; I believe the Lord Pro-
vost of Glasgow and other gentlemen ——"

John Douglas's face flushed quickly.

"I wish not to hear of such things," he said,
with a touch of resentment. Then he added
more slowly, "I will take money from no man.
I will earn my own living ; if I cannot do that,
what title have I to live at all ?   But I will take
this obligation from you yourself, Mr. Campbell ;

if you will lend me five pounds, which I will repay to you. And I would like to take with me a
few portraits, of my family and forbears, that
can be of no use to any one ; and one or two
books likewise ; then the rest can go to the
liquidators, to roup or scatter to the winds as
they see fit. I am a man of few words ; I will
repay you the money, if my health remains to
me ; and it will be enough to carry me to London
and start me there."

" To London ! " said the tall fair man in spec-
tacles.

" It is the great labour market of the world ;
it is natural I should go there. Besides, there
is another thing," he added, with a trifle
of embarrassment. " Our family were well
known in these parts in former years, and
respected. I know not what I may have to
turn my hand to. I will begin where I can be
alone."

He was a wilful man, and he had his way.
He got the five pounds and the few pictures,
and the three books named above ; and when he
entered the third-class carriage that was to bear
him through the night to London, it was without fear. He had ten fingers, and he could live

on a crust of bread and a drink of clear water. What was the hardship? Had not the great Emperor himself counted it among the blessings of his life—one of the things for which he was ever to be grateful—that he had been taught to work with his own hands?

CHAPTER II.

THIS, then, was the man who now found him-self in the sickly daylight of the great city, walking along the wide thoroughfare on this Sunday morning. The grim and grizzled face was somewhat tired-looking after the long and wakeful journey, and the dark eyes were fatigued and melancholy ; but his step was light and firm. And it was well that it was so. He had been in other large towns before, but not in this one ; and as he had determined to make for London Bridge, to get lodgings near there,—seeing that that looked on the map to be about the centre of the commercial district,—he had traced out the safest route, by Pentonville Road and City Road down to the Bank. As he trudged and trudged, however, and no Bank made its appear-ance, he gradually woke himself out of that dreamy and contemplative mood. He began to make inquiries about distance and so forth. The

driver of a four-wheeled cab, his purple bemud-
dled face lighting up with a dull sort of humour,
gave him a facetious invitation to get inside the
tumble-down old vehicle. The conductors of one
or two passing omnibuses hailed him; and he
gathered from their " Benk ! Benk ! " that at
least he was in the right direction. But he was
not going to spend money causelessly; so he
trudged on.

At length, when he got to the wide square front-
ing the Royal Exchange, the solitariness of the
place struck him with a strange chill. All the
great buildings closed and deserted ; not a habit-
able-looking house anywhere. But there were
numbers of people passing along the thoroughfares—mostly groups of young men of about
two-and-twenty, tallow-faced, round-shouldered,
wearing over-coats and billycock hats, and smoking short pipes ; and there were crowded omnibuses coming rolling along (what a difference
was this roar and rabble from the quiet of the
Sabbath morning far away there on the northern
coast !) and these people must live somewhere.
So again he contentedly trudged on ; down King
William Street ; over the bridge spanning the
misty river ; along the Borough Road ; until he

arrived at Union Street. He had so far failed
in his quest for lodgings ; but in Union Street he
espied a coffee-house ; and as he had become
both tired and hungry, he entered the dingy
little place, sat down, and ordered a cup of
coffee and a roll and butter.

It was a kind of shelter, after all ; though
everything was dreadfully dirty, and there was
a heavy odour in the place. The waiter, brought
him a greasy newspaper ; but he put it aside.
Then came his breakfast. The butter was
not touchable ; but he reflected that it was a
luxury which he, living on another man's
money, had had no right to order. When he
had paid back the £5, he would consider the
question of butter—though not butter such as
this. He ate the dry roll, and managed to
swallow the strangely-tasting coffee ; then he
fell asleep ; and was eventually wakened by
the ringing of church bells.

So, having paid his shot, he wandered out
again into the pale and misty sunlight ; and as
he had been struck by the appearance of St.
Saviour's in crossing the bridge, he strolled back
thither, and entered the church, and sat down in
a pew. He remained through the earlier part

of the service; but when the sermon began, he left. The streets were now quite busy, though the shops were closed. It was not like Sunday on the shores of the Firth of Clyde.

" In any case," he was thinking, "it can be no great breaking of the Sabbath that a man should provide himself with a lodging to cover his head."

Eventually, after much patient wandering and enquiring, he found a house in the Southwark-bridge Road—he was attracted to it by the presence of one or two flower-boxes on the window-sills—where he was offered a small, fairly neat and clean bedroom for the sum of three-and-sixpence per week. Thereupon the bargain was closed ; and John Douglas found himself established at least with headquarters from whence he could issue to fight his battle with the great forces of London.

Well, day after day—nay, week after week—passed, and all his efforts to obtain employment had resulted in nothing. It was not through any shamefacedness or fastidiousness or false pride. He was ready to do anything. Many people thought this man a maniac, who calmly walked in and offered, in his slow, methodic

Scotch speech, to copy letters for them, or do anything that could be pointed out to him, confessing, on interrogation, that he had been in no employment before, and could therefore produce no testimonials as to character or fitness. On his own showing, there was nothing special he could do; though he had bought a little treatise on book-keeping, and occasionally studied it in the evenings. As he walked about the streets and observed how all the people around him seemed to be fully occupied, and busy and contented, it occurred to him as strange that they should all have fallen into these grooves so naturally. He looked at the clerk giving out tickets at a railway station, and thought he could do that also. Perhaps the business of the young men who every morning were to be seen inside the big windows of the drapers' shops in the Borough Road, decorating the place with ribbons and gowns, demanded a special knowledge that he had not acquired; but it could not be difficult, for example, to be a policeman? They seemed happy enough; good natured; sometimes even with a word of chaff for the costermonger whom they ordered to move on, him and his barrow.

These not very anxious experiments, and quite idle speculations about the uses of various forms of labour, might have gone on indefinitely but for the very certain fact that Douglas's small stock of money was being slowly but surely exhausted. Slowly, it is true; for he had wholly given up tobacco; his dinner was a roll or a biscuit eaten in the street; and as his landlady charged him sixpence for each scuttleful of coals, he preferred to keep himself warm on these now bitterly cold evenings by tramping about outside and looking at the shops. That good woman, by the way, was sorely disappointed in this new lodger, out of whom she could make no indirect profit; and she had a waspish tongue. John Douglas regarded her taunts—almost amounting to open insult—with a patient and mild curiosity. It was a little bit of psychological study, and more interesting than bookkeeping by double entry. Meantime, things were becoming very serious; with all his penuriousness, he had arrived at his last half-sovereign.

CHAPTER III.

ONE night, a few minutes after nine, Douglas was returning home along one of the badly-lit little thoroughfares in the Borough, when he saw the figure of a woman slowly subside on to the pavement in front of him. She did not fall; she trembled on to her knees as it were, and then lay prone—near a doorstep. Well, he had grown familiar with the sights of London streets; but even if the woman were drunk, as he imagined, he would lift her up, until some policeman came along.

He went forward. It was not a woman, but a young girl of about seventeen or so, who did not seem a drunken person.

"My lass, what is the matter with ye?" he said, kneeling down to get hold of her.

"Oh, I am so ill—I am so ill!" the girl moaned, apparently to herself.

He tried to raise her. She was quite white,

G

and almost insensible. Then she seemed to come to; she struggled up a bit, and sought to support herself by the handle of the door.

"I shall be all right," she gasped. "I am quite well. Don't tell them. I am quite well— it was my knees that gave way——"

"Where do ye live, my lass?" said he, taking hold of her arm to support her; for he thought she was going to sink to the ground again.

"Number twelve."

"In this street?"

She did not answer.

"Come, I will help ye home, then."

"No, no!" she said, in the same gasping way; "I will sit down here a few minutes. I shall be all right. I—I am quite well——"

"Ye are not going to sit down on a doorstep on a night like this," he said, severely. "Come, pull yourself together, my lass. If it is number twelve, you have only a few yards."

He half-dragged and half-carried her along. He knocked loudly at the door. There came to it a tall, black-a-vised woman, who, the moment she saw the girl, cried out—

"Oh, Mary Ann, are you took bad again?"

"No—don't tell them," the girl said, as she

staggered into the narrow passage. "They'll turn me off. They said so the last time. I shall be all right. But my head—is so bad."

They got her into the dingy little parlour, and laid her down on the horse-hair covered couch. Her hand was clasped to her head, and her whole frame was shivering violently, as if with cold.

John Douglas, living that recluse life up there in the north, had never before had to deal directly with sickness, and he was terribly anxious and alarmed. What was he to do? His first wild notion, observing the violent shivering, was to order hot whisky-and-water ; then he thought it would be better to send for a doctor. But the tall, dark woman did not seem inclined to go or send for any doctor. She stood regarding the girl quite apathetically.

"Poor Mary Ann!" she said, watching her, as if she were a dog in a fit. "She wasn't took as bad as this before. She's been starving herself, she has, to keep her mother and her young sisters ; and she can't stand all day in the shop as she used to. I've seen it a-coming on."

"God bless me, woman," said Douglas, angrily, "we must do something instead of standing and looking at the poor lass. Cannot you tell me where the nearest doctor is? Has one been attending her?"

"Poor Mary Ann," the woman said, composedly; "she'll come out of it; but it's worse this time. A doctor? She couldn't afford to have a doctor, she couldn't. A doctor would be bringing physic; she can't pay for physic, she can't. She owes me three weeks' rent, and I ain't ast for it once, not once. Thirteen hours a day standing behind a counter is too much for a slip of a girl like that. Poor Mary Ann! Is your head bad, my dear?"

Douglas made use of a phrase which is not to be found anywhere in the writings of Marcus Aurelius, and hurriedly left the house. He made for the nearest chemist's shop, and asked the youth there where he should find a doctor. The youth glanced towards the back room, and said Dr. Sweeney was at hand. Dr. Sweeney was summoned, and appeared: a hard-headed-looking youngish man, whom Douglas immediately bore away with him.

The young Irish doctor did not seem much concerned when he saw his patient. He seemed to be familiar with such cases. He said the girl must be put to bed at once. She was merely suffering from a feverish attack, on a system weakened by exhaustion and fatigue. Then he began to question the landlady.

The usual story. Girl in a draper's shop; mother and sisters in the country; sends them most of her earnings; probably does not take enough food; long hours; constant standing; drinking tea to stave off hunger; and so forth. Douglas listened in silence.

"And when she recovers from this attack, slight or severe," he said at length, "what would restore that young lass to a proper state of health?—can ye say that, doctor?"

"I can say it easily," said the young Irishman, with a sarcastic smile. "I can prescribe the remedies; and there are plenty of such cases; unfortunately the patients are not in a position to follow my prescriptions. I should prescribe good food, and fewer hours of work, and an occasional week in the country air. It is easy to talk of such things."

"Ay, that is so," said Douglas, absently.

He went home. He took from his pocket the biscuit, wrapped in a bit of newspaper, that he had meant for his supper; but he put it on the top of a little chest of drawers, thinking it would do for his breakfast in the morning, and he would save so much. Then he went to the little stock of money in his locked-up bag, and found there eight shillings and sixpence. He took seven shillings of it, and went out again into the cold night, and walked along to the house where the sick girl was.

"Mistress," he said to the landlady, in his slow, staid. way, "I have brought ye a little money that ye may buy any small things the lass may want; it is all I can spare the now; I will call in the morning and see how she is."

"You needn't do that," said the tall woman. "Poor Mary Ann—she'll be at the shop."

"She shall not be at the shop!" he said with a frown. "Are ye a mad woman? The girl is ill.'

"She'll have to be at the shop, or lose her place," said the landlady, with composure. "There's too many young girls after situations now-a-days, and they won't be bothered with weakly ones."

CHAPTER IV.

A RESOLVE.

HOWEVER, as it turned out, there was to be no shop for Mary Ann the next day or for many a day to come. When John Douglas called in the morning, he was informed that she was "delirious-like." She was imploring the doctor—who had been there an hour before—not to let her lose her situation. She was talking about her mother and sisters in an incoherent way; also about one Pete, who appeared to have gone away to Australia and never written since. Douglas looked at the girl, lying there with her flushed face, closed eyes, and troubled breathing, unconscious of his presence, only twisting the bed-clothes about with her hot hands.

"Poor Mary Ann," the landlady said contemplatively. "If she dies, she'll 'ave to be buried by the work'us. And if she lives, she'll be worse off than ever; for they won't take a girl with cropped hair into a shop, and the fear of infection

besides. She ain't got a friend in the world, she
ain't ; except her own people, and they're only a
drain on the poor thing. Poor Mary Ann ! she
have had a bad time of it. Perhaps it would be
kinder in Providence if He took her ; for who's
to pay for her keep if she gets through the
fever ? Not that I would ask to be paid for her
lodging ; I ain't one like that ; there's her room,
and welcome ; that's what I says to my husband
when he come home last night ; and neither him
nor me's afraid of fever, nor would turn out a
poor thing as have been took. But law ! it
would be months afore she'd get another place ;
and she ain't got nobody to look after her. "

" What have you done with the money I gave
you last night ? " he asked.

" There it lies, sir—on the mantel-shelf. It
ain't for me to touch ; it is for the doctor to
give his orders about that money."

" Just put this eighteenpence to it, mistress,
and ask the doctor what the poor lass may want.
It is all I happen to have with me now."

Then he left ; and walked away with an
unusual air of determination. He was not
downcast because he had parted with his last
sixpence.

" It is even better thus," this stern-faced man
was saying to himself, "for now we must face
facts, and get rid of speculation. Let us begin
at the beginning—with one's ten fingers! Poor
lass! It is a dreadful place, a great city like
this ; it has no compassion. Surely, in the
country, she would not be so utterly thrown
down in the race. Surely, some one would say,
*" At meal-time come thou hither and eat of the
bread, and dip thy morsel in the vinegar ; "* and
would command the young men and say to them,
*" Let her glean even among the sheaves, and
reproach her not. And let fall also some of the
handfuls of purpose for her, and leave them,
that she may glean them, and rebuke her not."*
Poor lass! poor lass! Even that cadaverous-
jawed, Tennants'-stalk of a woman thinks it
would be better for her to die."

He walked quickly, his lips firm. It was a
miserable morning ; the noisy thoroughfares full
of mist and wet and mud ; drifts of sleet
swooping round corners ; the air raw and cold.
The river was scarcely visible when he crossed
London Bridge ; the steamers and ships were
like ghosts in the fog. He made his way as
quickly as he could through the crowded streets,

until he reached Tower Hill; then he passed up into the Minories; there he paused in front of one or two shops, in the windows of which were the most miscellaneous objects—old clothes, waterproof leggings, tin cans, and what not. At last he entered one of these places, and after a great deal of haggling and argument, he exchanged his coat of grey home-spun for a much shabbier-looking dingy blue over-coat, that appeared the kind of thing a pilot would wear. To this was added a woollen comforter; there was no money in the transaction. Douglas wrapped the comforter round his neck there and then, and put on the coat; when he stepped out again into the mud and snow and murky atmosphere, his appearance was much more reconcilable with the neighbourhood.

Still walking quickly, he went down to the London and St. Katherine Docks, passing under the shadow of the gaunt walls; and then along that dismal thoroughfare, Nightingale Lane, that looks like a passage between two great prisons; until at last, with moderate pace, and with a certain anxious, nervous look, as if he did not wish himself to be seen, he arrived at the entrance to a space at the corner of the London

Dock, which was enclosed with some rusted iron railings, and partially roofed over.

In this shed, shivering in the cold, and occasionally moving so as to avoid the whirling of the sleet, stood a number of most miserable looking wretches, men and lads. John Douglas knew very well who these were, and what they were there for. Here, so far as he had learned, was the only place in London where a starving creature could get work, without a character or qualification of any kind. Hither came those who, through drink, or idleness, or sheer misfortune, had got right down to the foot of the social ladder; waiting patiently in the dim hope that some extra pressure of work inside would occur to give them an hour or two's employment. Well, he did not hesitate long. He seized a moment when the attention of these poor devils had been attracted by some sound to the other side of the grating (where the foreman was expected to appear), and glided in among the group, hoping to be unperceived.

But what sharp eyes hunger makes! They had no sooner turned hopelessly away again, than every man and lad of them caught sight of the stranger. They did not resent his intrusion. They regarded him with curiosity, and with apathy. He looked well-to-do for that kind of work. Perhaps if he were one of the lucky ones, he would stand a pot of beer on coming out in the afternoon.

But to their great astonishment, they were all to be lucky ones that morning. The foreman appeared, ran his eye over the group, and engaged the whole of them for the day,—all except one dazed, drunken-looking tatterdemalion of sixty or so, whom he warned off by name. Almost before he knew where he was, John Douglas found himself at work in the docks, at fivepence an hour.

CHAPTER V.

TREASURE TROVE.

THE work was very easy, it seemed to him. What it might be in the warehouses he knew not; but here his business was simply to haul a small and light truck, carrying two boxes of oranges, from the unloading steamer along the side of the basin to the barge which was receiving them. The work was light, and there were pauses; moreover, the snow had ceased, and the surroundings—the ships and barges and what not—were picturesque enough; the scent of the oranges was pleasant. And his companions, these poor wrecks of humanity who had drifted into this curious, quiet little pool, were in the main good-humoured, though most of them seemed too depressed to speak much. Of course they instantly called him "Scottie." Scottie got through his short day's work with satisfaction; and when at four o'clock the great bell began to toll, and when his wages, two shillings

and a penny, were paid him, and when he set
out for the gate, he was much contented, and was
considering that, if he did his work diligently
and respectfully and in silence, it was not at all
unlikely that the foreman would take him on as a
regular hand, at four-and-twenty shillings a week.

He was thus thinking, and he had got almost
to the gate, when something ahead of him occurred that made him shrink back with a look of
dismay in his face. He saw that each man as
he passed through the portal held up his arms,
while one of the gatekeepers passed his hands
over his clothes. They were being searched.
Douglas stood still; his whole spirit in angry
revolt. He would rather give up his day's wage,
the coat off his back, the cap from his head—
anything than have to go through this shameful
ordeal. He looked back : could he not get out
by the wicket at which he entered, at the other
end of the docks ?

"Come on, Scottie ; you ain't been priggin'
oranges, eh ? " said one of his mates, laughing at
him.

Now it was quite clear that this searching of
the outgoing labourers was in most cases merely
formal ; but when the gatekeepers saw this man

hanging back, they naturally concluded he had been stealing. They called to him to come along. He hesitated no longer. With a grim air he advanced and held up his arms in the usual way. He would betray no shame. Doubtless it was a necessary precaution. And as he had stolen nothing, they could not hurt him by merely suspecting him.

But this gatekeeper's inspection was minute; and when he came to some slight protuberance on the breast of the coat, which, indeed, Douglas himself had not noticed, he demanded to know what it was. Nay, he had the coat taken off. On examination, a part of the lining of the coat was found to have been cut open and carefully sewn together again.

" Took all that trouble ? " said the gatekeeper, glancing at him.

" I did not know there was any pocket there," said Douglas, hurriedly; " I got the coat only this morning."

" Oh, indeed," said the other, with a slight derisive laugh. " I shouldn't wonder if we found some tobacco all the same."

The lining was ripped open, in the presence of the little crowd of labourers, carmen, stevedores, and so forth, who, seeing something unusual going on, had collected. Douglas certainly looked very guilty. His face was burning red; and the natural sternness of his features made him look as if he were angry at being detected. But, on the other hand, the expression on the face of the big yellow-bearded gatekeeper changed very suddenly, when he took from inside the lining a little oblong parchment bag, flat and dirty, and opened it, and drew out a thin packet of what turned out to be Bank of England notes. Not many, it is true; but a marvel all the same. The gatekeeper glanced at the culprit again, and said good-humouredly,

"Bought that coat this morning? Then you're in luck's way, my man, that's all I can say. We don't keep them kind o' goods in our warehouses. There ye are."

He once more examined the dirty little parchment bag all over; there was no scrap of writing on it, or on any of the notes.

"There ye are," he said, giving him back both the coat and the valuable package. "There's some as would advertise in the papers about that money; and there's some as would go to Scotland Yard, and expect to get something; and there's some, seein' as there's no writin', as would stick to it, and set up a shop. Where did you buy the coat, my man ? "

" At an outfitter's in the Minories—it was an exchange for my own," said Douglas hastily ; he was anxious above all things, money or no money, to get away from this crowd of curious faces.

" An outfitter ! yes, it's a fine name. Anyhow, the money don't belong to *him*. Most likely, now, that coat belonged to some seafaring man as got drowned, and the poor chap's things sold. Pass on there, my lads ! "

Douglas escaped from the crowd, and got away. He was greatly bewildered and excited ; not often in his life had he come through so much in so short a time. He walked hard, and did not stop until he sat down in his own little room, in the cold and dark.

Hour after hour he sat there, himself fighting with himself ; or rather his consciousness of what was right fighting with his great desire to do something to help that luckless child, lying there a few streets further off, friendless, poverty-stricken, fever-stricken, with the most hopeless of futures before her. He argued with himself

H

that no doubt the gatekeeper's guess was correct ;
the money had belonged to some sailor or pilot,
who had been drowned, and his personal effects,
whether found on his dead body, or perhaps in
the hold of a derelict, sold. Certainly these
notes did not belong to the old-clothes' man in
the Minories. It almost seemed as if a special
act of Providence had placed this money at his
disposal to succour this helpless one in her sickness, and support and strengthen her in her
convalescence. As for himself, he never dreamed
of touching it for his own uses. He had found
out at last one way of earning his own living.
But even if he were to be permanently employed,
at twenty-four shillings a week, how could he save
enough out of that to give this girl generous
nourishment, and a little wine, and country air,
when she should get well enough again ? In the
meantime, were her mother and sisters to starve ?
And it never occurred to him to ask why he
should take this sudden interest in this stranger
girl or in her family. The fact was, he had
never before been confronted with so clear a case
of hardship and distress. The solitariness, the
helplessness of the child appealed to him : it was
as if he had seen a wren threatened by a hawk,

or a rabbit seized by a weasel. He could not
help interfering, and doing his utmost.

And how could this money of a dead and
unknown man be put to a better use? Was he
to go and bury it in Scotland Yard? Was he to
advertise for a crowd of impostors to claim it?
He lit the gas and examined the notes. There
were seven—£35—a fortune! He saw the girl
in a little cottage, the window open to let the
first of the spring air into the room, she lying
well wrapped up on a couch, a few wild-flowers
on the table, daffodils and primroses from the
woods, pink-tipped daisies from the banks, the
red dead-nettle from the hedge-rows, and perhaps
herself, to please him, and out of gratitude as it
were, reading some of Tannahill's songs, 'Loudon's
bonnie woods and braes,' ' Langsyne, beside the
woodland burn,' 'Keen blows the wind o'er the
Braes o' Gleniffer,' 'We'll meet beside the dusky
glen on yon burn side.' Poor child! she had probably seen but little of the country during her
hard life. Would she be surprised when all the
hawthorn came out, and the lanes were scented?
Perhaps he would be able to teach her a little of
the beauty of simple things, and remove from
her mind the poor ideas about what is great and

admirable and desirable begotten in a large city. 'Consider the lilies, how they grow; they toil not, they spin not; and yet I say unto you that Solomon, in all his glory, was not arrayed like one of these.' No doubt her notion of what was most beautiful and desirable in the world was to be dressed in satin, and driving in a coach with powdered footmen behind, to a Royal Drawing-room.

All this was so specious and plausible. The money lying there seemed to belong to him more than to any other. And what good might be done with it ! Even if the real owner were alive, surely he would assent. Thirty-five pounds : ten pounds to be put into a savings bank in her name ; the rest to clear off the doctor's bill, give a weekly allowance to her people, and enable her to get a couple of months, or even more, with strict economy, in the country, before returning to the hard, dull work of London.

"I did not know," he said aloud, in his slow, deliberate Scotch way, " that money could have such value."

By-and-by he rose, put the notes into the bag again, and that in his pocket; then he turned off the gas and went out, thinking he would walk round and see how the girl was getting on. That is to say, he tried to make himself believe that that was all there was in his mind; but he knew very well that there was something else. There was a haunting, uneasy consciousness. Suddenly, at the corner of the street, instead of turning eastward as he should have done, he abruptly turned in the other direction, and began to walk quickly. "The money is not mine; I will have none of it," was his ultimate and fixed decision. "No dreams, man; no temptation. The first step to perdition is no doubt smooth enough. If I can do the lass a good turn, it must be with my own money."

He walked to Scotland Yard, finding it without difficulty, for he knew all the familiar features of London on the map; and there he told his story, and delivered up the money, and left his address. He departed with a light heart. Nay, when he had crossed Westminster Bridge again, he looked out for a poor-looking coffee house, and went in and had some coffee and a roll, and thought he never had enjoyed any dinner more. He looked at the evening paper, too, and then went out again into the wet streets, and continued his way. He was further cheered by hearing that the sick girl, though still feverish and perfectly weak and prostrate, had not, in the doctor's opinion, caught any serious malady, and only wanted time and care, and afterwards some better nourishment, to bring her round.

CHAPTER VI.

THE END OF THE EPISODE.

So with courage and patience, and with a final gulp about that searching business, he returned to his work at the docks, and very soon got engaged as a permanent hand. He was a favourite with the foremen, for he was industrious and minded his own business; but he was greatly disliked by his companions. They would not believe, and he was at no pains to convince them, that he had not kept the found money; and they had expected him, if ever he returned to the docks, to stand treat liberally. They were angry at Scottie's stinginess, and took to taunting him. These casual jeers he heeded no more than the idle wind; they could not hurt.

His savings slowly increased, his only serious expenditure being his weekly rent. When, each morning at twelve o'clock, the great bell rang in the docks, and the men and women came in

with their baskets and barrows, his dinner con-
sisted of a couple of penny sausage-rolls ("bags
of mystery," his mates called them), and these
were really quite fresh and clean and wholesome-
looking. In the afternoon or evening, he generally went round to the house where the girl,
Mary Ann Ellis, was now so far recovered that
she could sit propped up in bed for an hour or
so ; and he would have a chat with her and
her landlady, and a cup of tea, with bread
and butter—for which he privately paid. He
found this girl interesting, simple, and intensely
grateful, but ignorant to a degree that he had
not thought possible in a human being capable
of reading. In one respect this was lucky, for
she believed any nonsense he told her ; and the
quite imaginary associations of ladies and gentlemen for the dispensing of needful charity received her most earnest thanks for those little
sums that were sent to her mother, or that
enabled her to pay off her doctor's weekly
bill.

One day John Douglas was leaving the docks as
usual, when he was overtaken by a tall and hand-
some young fellow, whom he knew to be connected with the Customs department.

" I say, aren't you the man that found a lot of money ? "

Douglas had grown sulky, or rather suspicious of foolery, and was inclined to keep his own counsel.   But the accent of this stranger went straight to his heart ; he had not heard the Scotch way of speaking for many a day.   So he turned and regarded the young man, and frankly told him what he had done with the money.   This led to further questions, for the young man's curiosity was aroused.   It was the City of Glasgow Bank, then ?   But why take to such work as this ?   Couldn't he get into some office ?   Did he know a little of book-keeping ?

The upshot of all this was that, about a week after, John Douglas found himself installed as clerk at a tall desk in the back-room of a co-operative store connected with the docks, at a salary of two pounds a week ; and the first and immediate result of this was that the mysterious charitable associations of which he was apparently the agent, commissioned him to inform Mary Ann Ellis that she need not try to get any situation for at least two months' time, because fourteen shillings a week would be paid to her

during that period, to enable her to get tho·
roughly well again.

John Douglas grew to be a proud man. He was
proud of having paid off that five pounds, and
standing free of all the world ; he was proud of
his gradually-increasing account at the Government Savings Bank as a guarantee against future
ill ; but he was proudest of all of his patient,
whose convalescence he in a measure attributed
to himself. The days were longer now, and the
weather fine ; on the clear evenings, or Saturday afternoons, these two would get into an
omnibus, and go away out to Camberwell Green,
or Kennington Park, or Clapham Common, and
sit on a bench, and watch the young folks enjoy-
ing their sports and diversions. He was better
dressed now, and she had got into the way of
calling him " Sir." He told her a great deal
about Scotland, and the mountains, and the
glens with the birch-trees and water-falls ; but
he always got into a difficulty when he came to
the sea, which she had never seen. She could
not understand that.

" Now, lassie, look at that piece of water there,"
he would say to her, at the pond on Clapham
Common. " Cannot you imagine its going out

and out until it gets far beyond the trees and houses yonder, until it gets beyond everything, and meets the sky ? "

" I see what you mean, sir," she would say ; " but I can't understand it : for I can't help thinking, if there was nothing on the other side to hold it up, it must tumble down. How can water hold itself up in the air ? "

" Dear, dear me, lass ! " he would say impatiently, " have I not explained to ye how everything in the world, land and hills and everything, is held together ? "

" Yes, sir ; but water shifts so," she would say ; and he would take to something else.

The two months went by, and she got stronger and stronger, though sometimes she grew a little anxious about her chances of getting another situation. During this constant companionship, he had become much attached—in a compassionate sort of fashion—to this child whom chance had thrown in his way. He could see her good points, and her weak ones. She was of a kindly disposition ; truthful, he thought ; with no very distinct religion, but she had a general desire to be good ; simple and frugal in her ways of living, —though this was a necessity, and she had no

idea of frugality being in itself a virtue.   On the
other hand, her views as to what was most to be
desired in life were simply the result of the
atmosphere in which she had lived ; and she
confessed to him that the most beautiful thing
she had ever seen was the arrivals at a Mansion
House ball—the coloured stair-cloth, the beautiful ladies, the brilliant uniforms.   Her knowledge of politics was entirely derived from the
cartoons of the comic journals in the   shop
windows ; and she had any quantity of vague and
vulgàr prejudices about Catholics, Radicals and
Jews.   But this patient listener, who seemed
interested in her foolish little opinions, was a
largely tolerant man.   Such things were ; let
us make the best of them,—that was what he
seemed to say.   And as all the phenomena of the
universe appeared to him to be worthy of respect-
ful attention—even if one did not go the length
of vexing one's self about any one of them—he
was willing to learn that, in the opinion of this
profound observer, the Catholic priests were bad
men, who would let you do anything that was
wrong if only you paid them enough money for
absolution.

One evening, when he went round as usual, he

found Mary Ann in great excitement; she had evidently been crying, and now she was laughing in a half-crying way.

" What is the matter, lassie ? " said he severely, for he did not like " scenes."

" Oh, sir, Pete has written—at last—at last ! " she said, crying all the more, but in a glad sort of way, and looking again at the letter she held in her two hands.

" But who is Pete ? "

" My sweetheart, sir ; I never said anything about him—I thought he had forgotten us—but now he says he wouldn't write until he had good news, and now there is good news enough,—oh yes, there is ! there is ! For he has got a good place, and good prospects—and here is money to take me out and my mother and sisters, too—all except fifteen pounds, Pete says, and that he'll send in three months' time. Oh, sir ! you don't know what a good fellow Pete is ! "

John Douglas sat down. His heart felt a little heavy ; he scarcely knew why. But he began to ask a few questions, in a slow matter-of-fact way ; and he did not remain long. He saw that the girl wanted to read and re-read the good news to herself, and draw pictures of all that was coming.

The next afternoon Mary Ann got a note from him, with an enclosure. Thus it ran :—

"Dear Child,—You need not wait through three months of uncertainty. I enclose for you what will make up the passage-money, and also pay the expenses of your mother and sisters' coming to London. Accept this quietly and sensibly, and do not make any fuss about it, nor when I see you. I shall be busy this evening and may not call.

"Your friend,
"JOHN DOUGLAS."

But all the same Mary Ann came round quickly, and with her the tall, gaunt, dark, composed landlady ; and there was a great scene, Mary Ann crying and accusing herself of unheard-of stupidity for not having guessed that he all along had been her benefactor ; and he, on the other hand, sternly bidding her hold her peace and not talk foolishness.

"Ye did me a great service, ye foolish lass," he said ; " ye made me take to actual work when I was merely idling and loitering about. Ye gave me an object to work for, and pleasant companionship for a space, and now, if I must find something else, that is as it has been ordered; and I maun bide my time."

A few days afterwards he saw the mother when she arrived—a poor, limp sort of creature —and the two bewildered little girls. He could not, because of office work, go with them, as he had wished, to Southampton; but he accompanied them to the railway station, early in the morning, and bade them farewell. And as he turned away, he said to himself:

"These poor creatures I shall doubtless see no more in this world; but they will have a little regard for me, perhaps, while they live, and that is something. And now I will consider myself free to spend a trifle of money on myself, when I get it saved again; and I will use it during the holidays they speak of to take a trip back home again, and see the old place, and that the graves of my people are taken care of. And I may be able to make dispositions, too, so that when I am taken I may be placed there also; for it is but natural that one should wish to rest among one's own."

THE MAN WHO WAS LIKE

SHAKSPEARE.

THE MAN WHO WAS LIKE
SHAKSPEARE. ·

CHAPTER I.

THE DOCTOR DREAMS.

On the 24th of December last year Dr. Maurice
Daniel left his home in Brompton, London,
for his accustomed after-breakfast stroll. First
of all he walked down to Chelsea Bridge, and
had a look at the grey river, the grey skies, and
the grey shadows of London in the distance.
Then he wandered on until he found himself at
Victoria Station. Apparently having no business to do there—or any where else for the matter of that—he turned, and proceeded to make
the best of his way back to his own house.

Now it happened that he strayed into a somewhat narrow and dingy street, the narrowness
and dinginess of which he did not perceive, for
his mind was occupied with his familiar hobby,

which was phrenology. This hale old gentleman of sixty-five had himself some notion of completing the labours of Gall and Spurzheim, and had already collected some variety of materials in his odd little hermitage at Brompton. He was thinking of all these things in a somewhat absent way, when his attention was suddenly drawn to a small shop in this gloomy thoroughfare through which he was passing. It was a tailor's shop. There were no signs of a large trade in the place; in fact, one could only tell that it was a tailor's shop because the tailor himself was visible through the dirty window, seated on a board, and industriously plying needle and thread. It was the appearance of this man that had startled Dr. Daniel out of his reverie. The tailor bore an extraordinary resemblance to the Droeshout portrait of Shakspeare, insomuch, that the old gentleman outside could only stand and stare at him. There were points of difference, of course. The head was narrower than Shakspeare's, but the forehead was quite as lofty. The hair was red. What the tailor's eyes were he could not see, for they were fixed on his work; but they were probably light blue.

"Comparison and causality enormous," the

old Doctor said to himself. "Hope and wonder also large. Number and time deficient. Language, I fear, not much to speak of. But what a head—what a brain ! Fifty-five ounces, I will take my oath—six ounces over the average of the European male. Why, Lord Campbell had only fifty-three ; and then the splendid possibilities that lie in the difference ! What is Bain's phrase ? that " while the size of brain increases in arithmetical proportion, intellectual range increases in geometrical proportion." Here is a man with brain-power sufficient to alter the history of a nation."

The old Doctor walked on, dreaming harder than ever. And now there arose in his mind a project, of which the origin was two-fold. The night before he had been reading in his bachelor study a heap of Christmas literature, that had been sent him by his sister, an old maiden lady, who lived mostly at Bath, and who took this means of marking her friendly sentiments toward her brother. She was not a sentimental old lady, but she was correct and methodical in her ways, and believing that Christmas literature was proper at Christmas, she had despatched to her brother a fairly large quantity of it. Having

received the gift, he was bound to make use of
it ; so he sat down after dinner by his study fire
and pored over the stories, old and new, that she
had sent.   He began to feel that he ought to do
something for Christmas.   He did not wish to be
classed among those persons who, in the stories,
were described as sordid, mean, black-hearted,
generally villainous because they were indifferent about Christmas, or unable to weep over it.
Moreover, Dr. Daniel was really an amiable old
gentleman, and some of the stories of charity
touched him.   He was determined that nobody
should say he was a Mr. Scrooge, if only he had
an opportunity of doing anybody a good turn.

Now, as he walked home to Brompton this
forenoon, that vague desire of doing some bene-
volent deed co-operated with his deep-lying interest in phrenology to lead him to a daring
resolve.   Although not a very wealthy man he
was pretty well off, and always had sufficient
funds in hand for an exceptional call.   He would
now, he said, try what could be done with this
poor tailor.   He would give to that splendid
brain its opportunity.   Who could tell how
many village Hampdens and mute inglorious
Miltons had not been lost to this country simply

because we had no sufficient system of national education, by which the chance of declaring himself was elsewhere given to any capable youth? There could be little doubt but that the tailor was a victim to this lack of early instruction. In making his acquaintance, in becoming his patron, in placing before him opportunities of acquiring the power of expression, a good deed would be done to the poor man in any case, while there was also the beautiful and captivating hope that in course of time a great genius would reveal himself to his country, all through the kindly ministrations of a philosopher who should be nameless.

Inspired by this hope to overcome his natural shyness and timidity, Dr. Daniel came out again in the afternoon, and made his way down to the tailor's shop. The man still sat there—more ignoble drudgery could not be imagined. The Doctor entered.

" I did not observe your name over the door ? " said he, hesitatingly, to the tailor, who had turned quickly round, and was staring at him with a pair of small, piercing, light blue eyes.

" Tis Gearge O'Leary, Sor, " said the tailor, looking rather afraid.

The Doctor's hopes were slightly dashed : the man was an Irishman. But then, he instantly reflected, Ireland had not yet produced her Shakspeare ; perhaps this was he.

" An Irishman, I presume ? "

" Yis, Sor," said the tailor, somewhat recovering from his astonishment, and proceeding to get down from the board. " Is there anny thing, now, that—"

" Oh yes, " cried the old Doctor, immensely relieved to find a subterfuge suggested to him. " I wanted to see if you would repair some things for me. Dear, dear me, and so you are an Irishman ! I am sure I don't know what I wish done to them. Could you call this evening on me, about half-past eight ? Oh I don't wish you to work to-morrow—far from it ; but I should like to have the things taken away. Could you oblige me, Mr. O'Leary, by calling yourself ? "

That evening Mr. O'Leary, wearing an elegant black frock-coat, and a beautiful bright green neck-tie, was shown into the Doctor's study, where the old gentleman was seated by the fire, with a decanter of port and a couple of wine-glasses on the table.

" Now, Mr. O'Leary," said this cunning old

gentleman, with a fine affectation of manner, " I have my ways, you know, and I never do business with any man without having a glass of wine over it. Sit down and help yourself. 'Twas my grandfather left me that ; you needn't be afraid of it. And how long have you been a tailor, Mr. O'Leary ? "

" Is it how long I have been a tailor, Sor ? " said Mr. O'Leary, helping himself to the port, and taking care to have the glass pretty well filled ; " why, Sor, since ever I could spake, barrin' the five years I was in the army, until me father bought me out."

" You have been in the army, too ? Don't be afraid to try another glass of that port, Mr. O'Leary."

" Well, sure enough, 'tis Christmas-toime, Sor," said Mr. O'Leary, turning to the table right willingly.

Matters having been thus satisfactorily settled, the wily Doctor gradually began to get out of O'Leary all the facts concerning his history which he chose to tell. The Doctor's housekeeper had certainly brought in a number of old and shabby garments, which were flung on a sofa hard by ; but the Doctor made no reference to them, while his guest seemed sufficiently pleased to sit in a comfortable arm-chair, with a decanter of port wine at his elbow. Perhaps it was the wine that had made him a trifle garrulous; but at all events he talked about himself and his various experiences of life with a charming frankness. Here was a man, the Doctor said to himself, of infinite observation. Cuvier, with his sixty-four ounces of brain, could only stow away facts about birds, beasts, and fishes; here was a man, with probably nine ounces less, who had stored up invaluable experiences of mankind, their habits, customs, and humorous ways. O'Leary was as much at home among the fishermen of his native village, as among the democratic tailors of London. At one time he was describing his life in the army, at another telling how he had served as a gamekeeper when trade was bad. The more loosely his tongue wagged, the more daring became his epithets; but the Doctor was aware that Shakspeare himself had not always been cautious in his language. But when O'Leary came to describe his present circumstances, he grew less buoyant. Affairs were not going well with him. He could barely screw the rent of that humble shop out of his earnings. And then, with some shyness, he admitted the existence of a young woman who had a great interest in his welfare, and he said he thought they would never be able to get married if his small business did not improve.

"Ah, you have a sweetheart," said Dr. Daniel slyly. "I dare say, now, Mr. O'Leary, you have written some bits of poetry about her, haven't you?"

"Is it poethry?" said O'Leary, with a loud laugh; "'tis a mighty quare sort o' poethry, Sor, an' no mistake; but, oh yes, Sor, I've sent her many's the bit o' poethry, and 'tis very fond of it she is, Sor."

The old Doctor's face gleamed with delight; step by step the whole affair was marching on well. His fairest hopes were being realized.

"I have a great interest in literary matters, Mr. O'Leary, and I should like to see some of your poetry, but I fear I could not ask you to show me any of the verses you have sent to your sweetheart. Is there no other subject, now, that you have thought of trying? A man of your quick observation ought to aim at something better than sewing clothes. Do I speak too plainly?"

"Divil a bit," said Mr. O'Leary frankly.

"And, to tell you the truth, I should be glad to do anything in the way of helping you that I could. I don't say give up your trade at once; that is a dangerous step. To attain eminence in literature you require long and careful preparation—a wide experience that is only to be gained by diligent study of men in all walks of life—a freedom of expression only to be acquired by practice. And these things, Mr. O'Leary, are only the railway lines. The brain is the engine. You have got a good head."

"There's many a stick has been broken by coming against it, Sor," said O'Leary modestly.

"I do not wish to raise false hopes," continued the Doctor, feeling it his duty to express a doubt which he did not himself entertain for a moment; "but this I may say, that I am interested in you, and am willing to help you if I can. You may take these clothes, Mr. O'Leary, and look over them at your convenience. I am in no hurry for them. But if within the next few days you care to write a few verses, just to give one a notion of the bent of your mind and of your faculty of expression, I should be glad to see them."

" About what, Sor ? "

" Anything, anything," said the Doctor. " Obey the free impulse of your own imagination. By the time you see me again, I shall be able to tell you more definitely what I propose to do for you ; but in the meantime I think you ought to keep the matter to yourself. Do you understand me ? "

" Indeed I do, Sor," said Mr. O'Leary, getting up, and discovering that either the port-wine or the Doctor's plan had rather confused his head. However, he got the clothes together, thanked the Doctor most profusely, and left.

That night Dr. Daniel went to bed as happy as a man could be, and all night long he dreamed of brilliant receptions, of public meetings, of Queen's drawing-rooms, and more than all of his own great pride and glory in introducing to the world a new Shakspeare.

CHAPTER II.

THE FIRST TRIAL.

THREE days thereafter the Doctor received a letter, and as he opened it an inclosure dropped out. It contained Mr. O'Leary's first experiments in professional verse-writing. The Doctor seized it with avidity, and would have read it forthwith, but, being a methodical man, he placed it on the table, and read the letter first.

Mr. O'Leary was a bad penman ; it was with much difficulty that the old gentleman could make out the sense of the rambling lines. But when he did so, he was pleased. O'Leary confessed that he had not the impudence to bring his verses personally to the Doctor. He knew they were worthless. He was ashamed of them ; he even fancied he could do better. And then he added something about the condition of the Doctor's coats and trousers.

Here is the first composition, which the Doctor now proceeded to read, with some necessary alterations in Mr. O'Leary's spelling :—

" The moon was clear, the stars were white,
    The wind blew over the sea,
When Mary left her cottage home
    To go on board with me.

" Alas ! the ship was going fast,
    The storm did rage and roar,
And Mary stood upon the deck
    And look'd back to the shore.

" The moon was cover'd with the dark,
    The wind did blow aloud ;
She struck a rock and straight went o'er
    And all on board were drown'd."

" The poetry of the simple and uncultured mind," said the Doctor to himself, " naturally takes the lyrical form. Nations begin with *Chevy Chase* and end with *Hamlet*. In this artless composition the chief feature is its simplicity and directness of phrase. The stars are white ; the ship goes fast ; the girl, the central figure, stands upon the deck and looks back to the shore. It appears to me that there is genuine poetic sentiment in this very reticence of phrase, and in the stern sincerity and conciseness of the narrative. The professional critic, some disappointed poetaster, would remark, of course, that, '*drown'd*' does not rhyme with '*aloud*;' he would also make merry, doubtless, over the fact that if all on board were drowned, the narrator, being himself on board, would not have lived to tell the tale. But such is the criticism that stifles genius in its cradle. We cannot expect to have our young poets express themselves according to their inspiration, if we proceed to treat them with a godless banter. What I perceive in this composition of Mr. O'Leary's is a most promising naturalness and simplicity, coupled with a good deal of melody, especially, in the first verse. Let us see what he has done with his remaining effort."

Mr. O'Leary's second composition had evidently been written in compliance with a suggestion of the Doctor that a true poet should deal with the actual life around him—that he should tell us what he sees, and put into powerful verse the experiences, fears, and hopes of his fellows. Here it is:—

> "'Tis the grey of the evening in Vauxhall Road.
>   Alas! what sounds do I hear?
> A crowd is around the public-house door;
>   It is a quarrel, I fear.

He is drunk ; he doth lift up his hand !
In vain the policeman doth run !
Before he arrives the woman is struck down.
And all the mischief is done ! "

The Doctor was not sure about these lines. They contained, he reasoned with himself, a perfect picture of the scene which the poet had attempted to describe. But there was a lack of form, of method, of melody, apparent in the lines. They wanted the sweet idyllic charm of the verses describing Mary as she stood on the deck of the ship. But was he not himself responsible for this composition's failure? He had thoughtlessly discoursed to O'Leary about the virtues of realism. He had endeavoured to guide and direct the poetic instinct instead of leaving it free choice. Now the bent of O'Leary's mind was clearly synthetic and romantic ; he would not follow in the wake of Crabbe and Wordsworth. Doctor Daniel would omit further consideration of the lines about the Vauxhall Road. He would pin his faith to the charming ballad about Mary.

He sent a message to O'Leary that he wished to see him that evening. When O'Leary entered the study, he was inclined to be at once bashful

K

and nervous; but his patron speedily reassured him.

"You know," said he, with a smile, "you know, Mr. O'Leary, I did not expect you to be able to write poetry all at once. I merely wished to see if you had any leaning that way; and I must honestly say that there is a good deal of promise about the little ballad you sent me. Whether you may develope any very special gift remains to be seen, but if you care to make the experiment, I shall be willing, as I told you, to help you as much as I can. You must read and study the great fountain-heads of poetry; you must have leisure to go about and observe all varieties of men and things; you must have your mind relieved from anxiety in order to receive without dictation the materials for contemplation. I suppose you have a few books. Have you read Shakspeare?"

"Is it Shakspeare?" said O'Leary doubtfully. "Well, Sor, 'tis little I know av him in print, but sure I've seen him in the theatre. There's *Macbeth*, now, and the foightin' wi' swords; and as for the *Colleen Bawn*, 'tis a mighty foine piece intirely. Shakspeare, Sor? 'tis little av him I've seen mesilf; but he was a great man anny how."

"I see I must present you with a copy of his works, Mr. O'Leary. I may say, however, that Shakspeare did not write the *Colleen Bawn*, which is a modern piece, I believe. But first of all I think you ought to begin and study the ballad literature of our country; then you might proceed to Coleridge and Byron, and finally devote yourself to Shakspeare. You should also cultivate a habit of observation during your leisure rambles, not confining yourself to things which interest merely yourself. When you come to read Shakspeare, you will find how strangely he would enter into the opinions, sentiments, and aspirations of an ambitious monarch, and next minute how he could show himself familiar with the speech and thought of some common-minded peasant or justice of the peace. You must widen your atmosphere. You must forget Pimlico and Vauxhall Bridge Road occasionally. Now, if you had next Saturday free, I would myself go with you to Kew Gardens and Richmond; there you would see beautiful garden scenes and the quiet beauties of the river; while at Richmond you would see some of the grand houses of rich people, and observe something of their ways of living."

"Faix, it's mesilf would be deloighted to go wid ye," said O'Leary, with a rueful expression of face, "for 'tis little I'm doin' now with the shop; but little as it is, Sor—"

"Don't let that stand in your way," the old Doctor said generously. "I'm an old man, and have few claims on me in the way of friendship or benevolence. I told you I would give you an opportunity of rising to something beyond the sewing of clothes, useful and necessary as that occupation is. Now to put your mind at rest for at least this week, Mr. O'Leary, suppose I ask you to accept this little sum. Why I hope you don't misunderstand me? I believed you rather wished to enter into this project."

O'Leary was neither angry nor indignant; he was simply bewildered. He had received into the palm of his hand five golden sovereigns, and he could only stare at these in mute astonishment.

"Do ye mane it, Sor?" said he, fearing to put them in his pocket.

"Dear, dear me! it is no such great matter!" Dr. Daniel said, smiling at his companion's perplexity. "Put the money in your pocket, Mr. O'Leary. It is Christmas-time, you know, when the giving of little presents is permissible."

" Am I to write anny more poethry, Sor ? " said O'Leary, putting the sovereigns in his pocket.

" If you have any impulse that way, I should be glad if you would trust to it. But in any case you will call on me at ten next Saturday morning ? "

" That I will, Sor ! " said O'Leary, not quite sure but that this was all a dream.

When he got outside, he went to a lamp, and took out the sovereigns. Sovereigns they certainly were ; and yet he was puzzled. He went into a public-house and had a glass of ale, in order to have one of the golden coins changed ; the man gave him a heap of silver in return. He came out again with a lighter heart.

" Bedad," said he to himself, " and 'tis a poet I am. Me mother knew nothin' about it ; me father, rest his sowl, was accustomed to bate me if ivver I'd a pen in me hand. But what would they say to thim blissed five gowld pieces, and all for a dirthy scrap o' writin'? Oh, 'tis a moighty foine thing to be a poet, an' no mistake. And now 'tis to Biddy I'm goin' ; and will she belave it ? "

CHAPTER III.

A CONSPIRATOR.

Now there was not anywhere in London a more amiable, simple-minded, and pious young woman than Biddy Flanagan, who was the poet's sweetheart. She was a domestic servant, rather good-looking, with a fair, freckled face, hair nearly as red as her lover's, and a brogue much less pronounced than his. But when O'Leary told this poor girl all the story of his adventure with Dr. Daniel, her quick invention and pathetic hope rather got the better of her conscience. She did not tell her sweetheart that she considered Dr. Daniel a good-natured old maniac, but she acted on that assumption. By this time, be it observed, O'Leary had begun to share in the Doctor's illusions or aspirations. He showed Biddy copies of the verses he had written, for which she professed a great admiration, though she could not read them very accurately. But after O'Leary had described the Doctor's project, and shown her the four gold sovereigns and the silver, and talked about the holiday at Kew, and so forth, then she gave him, with an artful ingenuousness, her advice.

It was this. Her sweetheart, she faintly hinted, might in time turn out to be a great man, and that would be a fine thing for him at least. As for her, she could not expect him to go out walking with her after he had been to grand houses. On this, of course, O'Leary protested that whatever rank and wealth might fall to his lot, he would never desert the girl who had remained true to him so long and waited so patiently for that better fortune which seemed now to be approaching. Biddy, continuing, gently reminded him that rich people might be fickle in their patronage, and might not care to wait for years to see the end of their projects. O'Leary had written two poems; the result was 5*l*. Would it not be better to continue writing these as rapidly as possible, so that as much ready money as Dr. Daniel might be willing to give could be secured at once? And then, if her sweetheart did care about getting married—

The suggestion was not lost on O'Leary. After all, he reflected, however great were the

possibilities of the future, a little money just
now and a marriage with his faithful Biddy were
far more attractive.

"But divil the bit can I think of anny thing
more to write," said her sweetheart. "'Tis a
moighty hard thing, the writing of poethry ; and
that's the truth, Biddy darling."

"Arrah, now," said Biddy impatiently, "what
harm would there be in taking a bit here or
there, just to keep up the gintleman's spirits,
and by-and-by 'tis many a fine bit of poethry
you'll give him into the bargain, when it comes
aisier to ye."

"There's something in that, Biddy," said
O'Leary, not only listening to the tempter, but
anxious to find reasons for agreeing with her.
"'Tis mesilf that knows that ye can't make a
pair of throwsers till ye've learned to thread the
needle, and sorra a bit do I know of the making
of poethry. But, Biddy, d'ye see, if he was to
come on the poethry—"

"What !" cried Biddy, "an ould gintleman
like that ! 'Tis not a loine of our good ould
Irish songs will he know ; and 'tis no chating
of him, Gearge dear, for you'll make it up to
him whin the writing of your own poethry

comes in toime. Now there's the *Cruiskeen Lawn*—"

"Get along wid ye, Biddy!" said O'Leary rather angrily ; " and is it a fool you'd make av me ? Why, the old gentleman has been to all the plays and the theatres, and isn't it out av the ould songs like that that they make the plays!? Sure and it's the police-office I'd foind mesilf in, and not in Kew Gardens at all at all."

" There's manny more," said Biddy shrewdly, not pressing the point.

O'Leary pondered over this suggestion for a day or two. He did not think he would be really imposing on the old gentleman by occasionally quoting a verse from some one else as his own. It was merely borrowing to be repaid back with interest. At some future time, when the writing of poetry had become easier to him, he would confess the true authorship of these verses, get them back, and offer in their stead large and complete poems.

He dressed himself very smartly to call on Dr. Daniel on that Saturday morning. He had even gone the length of getting a tall hat—an ornament which he seldom wore, because the peculiar shape of his head made it almost impossible for him to wear such a hat with safety, especially if the day were windy. The Doctor was glad to see him; the morning was a pleasant one ; they both set out in an amiable frame of mind.

In the railway carriage O'Leary took a piece of paper from his pocket. His guilty conscience revealed itself in his forehead—that lofty forehead that had caused the old Doctor to dream dreams. The colour that appeared in his face Dr. Daniel took to be an evidence of modesty ; and is not all true genius modest ?

"So you have been busy again," said his Mentor, with a pleased smile. "You must not write as if you wished to gratify me. It is your own future of which I am thinking."

He read the lines, which were these :—

> "As charming as Flora
> Is beauteous young Norah,
> The joy of my heart
> And the pride of Kildare !
> I ne'er would deceive her,
> For sad it would grieve her
> To know that I sigh'd
> For another less fair."

"Very pretty—very pretty indeed," the Doctor said approvingly, and O'Leary breathed again. "There is much simple melody in the verse; and the ending of it, taking it for granted that any other must be less fair than she, is quaint and effective. Did you say your sweetheart's name was Norah, Mr. O'Leary?"

"Biddy, Sor," said his companion.

"That is not quite so poetical," said the Doctor; and then he continued the reading :—

> "Where'er I may be, love,
> I'll ne'er forget thee, love,
> Though beauties may smile
> And try to ensnare;
> But ne'er will I ever
> My heart from thine sever,
> Dear Norah, sweet Norah,
> The pride of Kildare !"

"Very good—very good also," said the Doctor; "although there is just a touch of self-conscious vanity—you will excuse me, Mr. O'Leary—in the notion that beauties would endeavour to ensnare the hero of the lines. But perhaps I am wrong. You do not write these lines as the utterance of yourself. The poem, so far as it goes, is dramatic—an impersonation. Now the majority of men, when they are young, are vain enough to believe that beauties do try to ensnare them : hence the sentiment expressed by this person is, I believe, true ; and I beg your pardon."

At this point, it must be admitted, O'Leary's conscience was touched. He felt that it was a shame to impose on this good-natured and generous old gentleman. He could almost have thrown himself on his knees on the floor of the carriage, and confessed that he was a scoundrel and a knave.

Some recollections of Biddy, and her pretty, honest, anxious face prevented him. The poor girl had waited patiently for that better luck which never came. The milkman had offered to walk out with her, the postman had offered to marry her this very Christmas, but she had remained true to the hapless tailor, on whom Fortune seemed resolved to send not the briefest ray of her favour. And now when he saw within his reach a means of bettering himself somewhat, and of releasing her, from the bondage of that overcrowded house in Lambeth to give her a couple of rooms—small, indeed, but her own— he tried to stifle that feeble protest of his conscience. He saw Dr. Daniel fold up the paper and put it in his pocket-book; and he knew that the die was at length cast.

All that day the friendly Doctor took his pupil about, showing him how differently different people lived, pointing out the beauties of the grey and wintry landscape, and talking to O'Leary of how he should set about his self-education. In the evening the poet dined with the Doctor, much to the amazement of the old housekeeper, who was indignant, but silent. At night he went away with a whole armful of books.

Next evening he saw Biddy, and he was in a downcast mood.

"Biddy," said he, "'tis moighty afeard I am we are thieving from the good ould gintleman. There is another five pounds to come to me next week; and, bedad, the mate that I'll buy with it'll go near to choking me, it will."

Biddy was for a moment a little frightened; but presently she said,—

"And is it you, Gearge O'Leary, that would be setting yourself up as a better judge of poethry than the ould gintleman, and him a Doctor too? And if it is the poethry he wants, can't ye give him enough of it in toimes to come, and a good pennyworth over, so there'll be no repentin' of the bargain betune ye? And, indeed, it is not another year, Gearge dear, that I could stop in that house. What with the noine children, and the washin' all day, and the settin' up for the masther till three in the mornin', 'tis me coffin next you'll be for buying, Gearge dear, and not anny wedding-ring."

O'Leary's doubts were banished for the moment, but not destroyed.

CHAPTER IV

FOREBODINGS.

IT must be said for O'Leary that he honestly did his best to requite the Doctor's care. He devoted every minute of his leisure time to that self-education which had been recommended to him; he industriously laboured at the books which had been given him. Somehow or other, however, the big brain behind that splendid forehead would not work. When he tried to understand certain things the Doctor told him, in explanation, a sort of fog appeared to float before his eyes. When he tried to write verses of his own composition, blankness surrounded him. He would sit helplessly by his table for hours, no suggestion of any subject occurring to him. He grew irritable and impatient. The Doctor noticed that his pupil, when they walked out together, had lost much of his old gaiety of spirits. He began to wonder whether tailoring

and study combined were not proving too much
for O'Leary's health.

Otherwise all seemed to go well with him.
The old Doctor was as much in love with his
project as ever, and had grown to take a very
keen and personal interest in the affairs of this
poor man. Finding out that much of O'Leary's
anxiety was apparently connected with the
question of his marriage, he suddenly resolved
upon setting his friend's mind at rest on that
point by an act of exceptional generosity. He
told O'Leary that he evidently wanted change of
air and scene. When he got married he would
have to leave his present humble lodgings. Now
what did he think of living a few miles out of
London—say about Hammersmith or Barnes—
where the Doctor would purchase for him a small
cottage, and furnish the same? The walk in of
a morning would improve his health, and afford
him ample time for thinking. If he would see
Biddy Flanagan, and arrange about the marriage,
the Doctor would proceed forthwith to seek out
and purchase some small cottage.

When he told Biddy of this proposal there
were tears in his eyes.

"Biddy," said he, "'tis a jail and not a cottage

that I'm fit for. Sure there's not a day I go up to the ould gintleman's house now that I'm not trimbling from me head to me foot—with shame, yes, with shame. Biddy, what o'clock is it?"

" 'Tis after ten, I belave."

" This very minnit I'll go and tell him what a rogue I've been," O'Leary said, stopping short on the pavement.

The girl looked at him, frightened and silent; but her hand was on his arm, and he did not move. Then she spoke to him. She did not attempt to justify what had been done ; she only pleaded that, now it was done, he should wait and accept this cottage—as a loan, not a gift. They would be most economical. She knew how to tend a small kitchen-garden. She would take in washing. O'Leary would save up what he could in the shop, and then by and by he could go to Dr. Daniel, confess his forgeries, and pay the first instalment of the money which he had to refund. Dr. Daniel had already given him 20*l*. in money, besides an immense number of books; they would accept this climax of his generosity, and being installed in the cottage, would work faithfully to pay back the whole.

L

O'Leary consented, with evil forebodings in his mind, and resumed his imposture. He had almost began to despair of ever being able to do anything himself; he did not even try now; he merely copied a verse or two of one of Moore's songs, and took that to the Doctor to encourage the old gentleman's hopes. Fortunately Dr. Daniel showed none of these contributions to his friends. They had got vaguely to know that he had recently picked up some odd protégé; but the Doctor was not communicative on the point, wishing to have some finished work of O'Leary's before introducing him to the world.

But each time that the tailor copied out some verses and carried his stolen wares to the house in Brompton, he grew more and more agitated. A feeling of sickness came over him as he rang the bell; when he came away, he felt inclined to walk down to Chelsea Bridge and end his anxieties in the river. The remorse that he felt seemed to be increased by each fresh proof of the old Doctor's generosity, while the fear of detection became almost unbearable. He grew haggard in face. He was peevish and irritable, so that Biddy was almost afraid to speak to him when they went out walking together. At last, one night, he turned and declared to her fiercely, that it was all her fault, and that she had made a thief of him.

The girl burst out crying, and spoke in a wild way of drowning herself. She quitted him abruptly, and walked off in the direction of the bridge.

For some time he gloomily regarded her, uncertain what he should do ; then he ran after her and stopped her. He would do what she wanted. He would say nothing more about the whole affair till they had the cottage. So he gradually pacified her ; but from that moment each felt that the mutual confidence which had existed between them had suffered a serious shock, and that at any moment something might occur to sunder it altogether.

So the days and weeks went by. The small cottage was at last got hold of ; and so great was the interest of the Doctor in this project, that he sent for his sister to come up from Bath to help him in selecting some pieces of furniture and the necessary saucepans and dishes. Should O'Leary turn out to have the poetical power which the shape of his head promised, might not this little cottage come to be in future times regarded with interest by travellers from all parts of the world ?

But the near approach of this marriage, and the prospect of possessing this tiny residence, did not seem greatly to raise the spirits of O'Leary and his betrothed. Biddy now began to look anxious too—anxious and apprehensive, as if she lived in constant dread of something happening. She made fewer appointments with O'Leary ; sometimes they walked for an evening together with scarcely a word passing between them. The old delight of their meetings had passed away,

One night he was to have met her, but he did not come—a most unusual circumstance in his case, for he was a dutiful lover. More strangely still, no word of explanation came next morning. All the next day she waited and worried, harassed by a hundred fears ; and at last, in the evening, she went to her mistress and begged to be set at liberty for a couple of hours. The request was sulkily granted.

Rapidly indeed did she run across the bridge and up through the gaunt and silent streets of Pimlico. With a beating heart she knocked at the door of .O'Leary's lodgings ; the landlady, who knew her, came. She had scarcely breath left to ask if Mr O'Leary was at home. The landlady, a fat, good-natured shabbily-dressed woman, drew her inside, and motioned her to keep quiet.

"He was took werry ill yesterday, the poor young man, in a fever like, and to-day he has been wandering. There's something on his mind, miss, that is troubling the poor young man— about them books he has, and some money ; and law ! the way he has been goin' on about you ! But I knew as you was sure to come over this hevenin'—and will you go upstairs ? "

Biddy followed the landlady upstairs as if she was in a dream. In a bewildered sort of way she saw the door opened before her, and found herself being taken noiselessly into the small room, which was dimly lit with a solitary candle. In the bed in the corner O'Leary lay, apparently asleep, with a bright flush in his face. He turned round uneasily ; he stared at her, but did not recognize her ; then he turned away again, muttering something about Dr. Daniel and Chelsea Bridge,

Biddy seemed to recover herself. She went

deliberately over to the bed, her face pale and determined, and said,—

"Gearge, me darlin', don't ye know 'tis me? Where's the money? Give me the money; and 'tis every farden av it and every blessed wan o' the books that I'll take back to the Doctor this very minnit. Don't ye hear me, Gearge dear?"

The sick man groped underneath his pillow, and feebly brought out a leather purse. He gave it her, without looking at her, and said,—

"Take it all back, Biddy."

The landlady could not understand the fierce look of determination on the girl's face. Biddy put the purse in her pocket. She gathered up the books from the corner of the room, piled them on the table, and then whipped the table-cover round them, and tied up the ends. With this heavy load on her back she staggered downstairs, and along the narrow passage.

"'Tis the books and the money have brought the fever on him," she was muttering to herself; "wirra, wirra, but 'twas a bad day that he met that ould gintleman, wid his books and his money. And sure, whin I give him them back, 'tis to Father Maloney I'm goin', to tell him that Gearge O'Leary is down wid the fever."

CHAPTER V.

The Doctor's sister came up from Bath—a thin, precise little woman, with silver-grey curls and shrewd grey eyes. She wanted to know more about this protégé of her brother's, of whom she had vaguely heard. Thereupon the Doctor, forgetting his shyness, grew quite garrulous about his project, described O'Leary's magnificent forehead, told her all that he hoped from it, and said that already he had received ample proofs of the man's poetical leanings. To all this Miss Daniel listened attentively, but silently. When he had finished, she asked him if she might look at some of Mr. O'Leary's pieces.

The Doctor was at first inclined to refuse. It would be unfair to take these compositions as evidence of what O'Leary might hereafter do. But Miss Daniel was so firm in demanding to see some actual work of the new poet's, that her brother at last consented to go and fetch some of it.

She had scarcely begun to read the first of the pieces when he observed an extraordinary expression come into her face. She stared at the paper; then a flush of anger appeared on her forehead; finally she looked at himself with something nearer contempt than pity.

"How can you, Maurice," she said to the frightened Doctor, "how can you let people make a fool of you so? Year after year it is always the same—some new craze, and some new impostor taking advantage of you. Last year it was those relics of Sedan : they were no more relics of Sedan than I am. Why, don't you know that this man has been palming off on you verses of Moore's songs—songs that every school-girl knows? Oh yes, your Mr. O'Leary is not a fool ; his big forehead can do something for him."

The Doctor would not believe it. He was inclined to be violently angry. Then his sister walked out of the room.

In a few minutes she returned. She had managed to unearth an old copy of "Moore's Irish Melodies," which she had left in the house in days gone by. Without a word she opened the page, put her finger at a certain passage, and placed it before her brother. Doubt was no longer possible. Here was O'Leary's "Oh, believe me, if all those endearing young charms;" there was Moore's version of the same. Miss Daniel rapidly ran over O'Leary's manuscripts. She could identify nearly all the pieces, though some of them were disguised. The very first of them—that which described Mary standing on the deck of the doomed ship—she declared was stolen from a Scotch song.

It was really some time before the full sense of O'Leary's perfidy was impressed upon the good old Doctor. He showed no signs of anger; but he was deeply pained and humiliated. It was not so much that his own pet scheme had fallen through, but that one whom he had tried to benefit should have betrayed him so grossly.

Miss Daniel was of another mind. She demanded to have the man punished. She insisted on the Doctor, although it was nearly ten o'clock, taking her to see this traitorous tailor, so that he might be confronted, and his ingratitude and meanness pointed out to him. She talked of a policeman, and the crime of obtaining money on false pretences, her brother all the while listening in a confused and absent way, as if he did not even yet understand it all.

At this moment Dr. Daniel's housekeeper tapped at the door, opened it, and announced that a young woman called Flanagan wished to see the Doctor, having a message from Mr. O'Leary.

A gleam of virtuous indignation leaped into Miss Daniel's eyes; she bade the housekeeper show her in at once.

The next moment Biddy Flanagan, still with something of a wild look in her face, entered the room. She did not see that there was any stranger present. She hastily undid the table-cover placed the heap of books on the table, and counted out beside them eighteen sovereigns; and then she turned to the Doctor.

"Thim's the books, Sor," she said, in an excited way, "and there's the money—all but two of the gould pieces annyhow, and to-morrow you'll have thim too—and sure 'tis the light heart I have in putting thim there. And. the cottage, Sor—plaze your honour, we'll have nawthin' to do with the cottage—"

"My good girl, what is all this about? What do you mean?" the Doctor said.

"What do I mane?" Biddy cried, with her lips getting tremulous and her eyes filling with tears, "why, 'tis George O'Leary, Sor; he's down wid the fever; and what has brought the fever on him but the books, and the money, and all the chatin'? and 'twas me that did it, Sor; indeed it was mesilf, and not him at all; and the poethry, Sor, he brought you, sure 'twas all stolen; and I made him do it, for 'twas the weddin' I was thinkin' of—"

Here Biddy burst out crying; but she quickly recovered herself, and made some wild effort to express her contrition. She had no time to lose. She was going off for Father Maloney. It was the ceaseless anxiety, she explained, about the imposture that had worried her lover into a fever; now she had brought them back, and confessed her fault, she was going to fetch the doctor and the priest.

When she had left, Miss Daniel said to her brother,—

"Will you go and see this poor man?"

"To upbraid him when he is down with a fever?" said the Doctor indignantly.

"No; to relieve his mind by telling him you forgive him. And you have not a great deal to forgive, Maurice. You must have driven the man into deceiving you. Suppose you were to tell him now—or as soon as he can understand you—that you don't wish him to earn that cottage by writing poetry, but that you will give it him as soon as he is well enough to get back to his tailoring ; don't you think that would help to get him better ? "

It did ; and George and Biddy are at this moment installed in the cottage, the latter quite contented that her lover should not have turned out a great poet, and he glad to be relieved from a task which was too much even for his magnificent brain. As for the old Doctor, he has not given up his faith in phrenology, of course, merely because · it apparently failed in one instance. He has still a lingering suspicion that O'Leary has thrown his opportunity away. However, if the world has lost, O'Leary has gained : there is not a happier tailor anywhere.

THE STRANGE HORSE OF LOCH SUAINABHAL.

THE STRANGE HORSE OF LOCH SUAINABHAL.

———◆◇◆———

THE following is a copy of a letter addressed to a lady living in Hyde Park Gardens, London, by Alister-nan-Each, of Borvabost, in the island of Lewis, Hebrides :—

BORVABOST, *the 20th of June*, 1875.

HONOURED MADAM AND DEAR MISTRESS
TO COMMAND,

You waz writen to Alister Lewis, the school-master, that I would tell you the whole story of the Black Horse I sah at Loch Suainabhal ; and I am not good at the writen whatever ; but I will tell you the story, and I will tell you from the verra beginnin of it the whole story. It waz John the Piper he will go about tellin a foolish tale about me ; and it waz many a time I will think of going and breaking his pipes over his head, that he will tell such foolish lies. There

is no man in the island will drink more az John
the Piper himself, not one ; and so you will not
belief his foolish lies if you will be hearin of
them, Miss Sheila.

Now the verra beginnin of it waz this, that
Dugald MacKillop, that lives by Loch Suainabhal, and his father waz my wife's father's first
cousin, ay, and a verra rich man mirover, for he
had more az forty pounds or thirty-five pounds
in the bank at Styornowa, he will be going away
to Portree to marry a young lass there, and
Dincan Peterson and me would be for going with
him too, and I waz to be the best man. And
you will not mind John the Piper's lies, Miss
Sheila, for it waz only one gallon of good whisky
we took aboard the *Clansman* steamer when we
waz going away to Skye—as sure as death it
waz only the one gallon that Dincan and me we
waz for taking to the young lass's father—but it
waz verra wat on board the boat, and verra cold
whatever, and what harm is there in a glass of
the goot whisky ? Sez Dincan Peterson to me,
he sez, Alister, there is plenty of goot whisky in
Skye, and what for should we keep the whisky ?
and both me and Dugald MacKillop the two of
us both together said he waz a sensible man, and

not a foolish man, like John the Piper. And it waz only the one gallon in the char we had on board the steamer.

I will tell you now, honoured Madam, that the wonderful big ship took us quick to Portree, which is a great distance away; but we did not go to bed that night, for there waz two or three waiting for us, and we had a glass mirover and a dance or two. And the next morning we went away to the farm where the young lass waz; and that was among the hills; and there waz never in the world such rain as there is in Skye. Ay, in the Lews we have the bad weather, and the goot weather; but Gott knows there is no such watter falling anywhere az there is in Skye; but we had a glass and a dance, for the two pipers waz with us; and in the evening of that day there waz a grand supper at the young lass's father's house. And it was not ten gallons of whisky we took in the cart; and Gott knows I will mek John the Piper answer for that some day; but only six gallons; and there waz a goot many people there for a dance and a song. And there waz no one wished to go to bed that night either, for there waz many people in the house, and a good dram and a dance for every one;

M

and the way the two pipers played the pipes that night would hef made a dead man jump in his grafe if he had been dead for two hundred years, ay, or one hundred years mirover. And you will mind, Miss Sheila, that the story about the ten gallons of whisky is only the lies of that foolish man, John the Piper, who is trunk oftener az any man on the island of Lews.

The next day waz the day of the marrach; and who is there will not tek a glass at the marrach of a young girl? And after the marrach we went away to this house and to that house, and the two pipers playing in the front of us verra fine, and many a dance we had, ay, and the old people too, when they had got a goot tram. And in the evening there waz another peautiful supper; and no less az six and twenty hens, and cocks, and chickens, and rabbits, all boiled together in the boiler for boiling the turnips; and the big barn with more az twelve or sixteen, or more az that of candles; and it waz a peautiful sight. And if the father of the young lass will send to Portree for so many, or so many gallons of whisky, what is that to any one, and to one mirover that waz not there, but will only mek lies about it? I will not interfere with any man's whisky; no, and I would not go and tell foolish lies about it mirover.

There waz one or two of the old people, they will go to bed in the cart that night; and there waz good hay on the ground, and the cart upside down to keep away the rain; but the most of us we waz for no sleepin that night, for a young lass does not get marriet every day. And in the morning Dugald MacKillop and the young lass they will come out to us; and they would hef us trink their verra goot health before he went in to the fresh herrings, and the milk, and the cakes; and when that waz all over, we had the pipers to the front of us, and we set away for Portree. And who would not trink a glass, when you call at this house and at that house, to let a young lass say good-bye to her friends? And all the way to Portree there waz this one and the other one come out to shake hands with the young lass; and many of them came down to the big steamer to see her away. And as for Dincan Peterson and me, there waz one or two on board of the big steamer that we knew; and we had a glass or two with them whatever, for it waz a verra cold night; but the lies of that foolish man, John the Piper, are more as I can

understand. I will not say, Miss Sheila, for it
is the old story I will be telling you, that Dincan
Peterson and me we were not verra tired when
we got to Styornowa; for it waz five nights or
more we waz not in any bed at all; but there
waz two or three of our friends will meet us at
Styornowa to drink a glass to Dugald MacKillop
and the young lass, and who would be thinkin
of going to bed then? No, nor waz there any
more thinkin of going to bed when we got to the
farm of Dugald MacKillop by Loch Suainabhal;
for there waz two or three come to see the young
lass he had married; and it was Aleck Cameron,
that lives by Uig, he had brought over two
gallons of verra goot whisky—or perhaps, Miss
Sheila, for I will tell you the whole story that
you will see what lies old John the Piper would
be for telling—perhaps it waz three gallons. I
cannot mind, now; but it waz of no consequence
whatever; and to go about speaking of men
being trunk that has just drunk a glass or two
at a marrach, is no more az foolish and wicket
nonsense.

It was the day after this day that Aleck
Cameron he sez to me, "Alister, you hef not
been to Uig for many a day; will you go back

to Borva by the way of Uig; and we will go
together, and we will hef a glass at Uig." And
I said to him, " It is a long time, Aleck Cameron,
since I will be at Uig, and I will go with you,
and we will drink a glass with your father and
your mother before I will be going on to Borva."
And it waz about fife o'clock in the afternoon
when we set out; but Aleck Cameron he is the
most quarlsome man in the whole of Lews; ay,
there is no one, not even John Fergus himself,
will be so bad in the temper as Aleck Cameron;
and what did he know about the Campbelton
whisky? I hef been in Isla more as three times
or two times myself; and I hef been close by
the Lagavulin distillery; and I know that it is
the clear watter of the spring that will mek the
Lagavulin whisky just as fine as the new milk.
And the bottle I had it waz the verra best of the
Lagavulin; and I sez to him, " Aleck Cameron,
if you do not like the whisky I hef, you can go
back to the farm of Dugald MacKillop, and you
will get what whisky you like; and you are a
verra quarlsome man, Aleck Cameron." And he
is a coarse-speakin man, Miss Sheila, and I will
not be writen to you the words that he said;
but he went away back to the farm whatever;

and I kept on the way by myself, without any
bread or cheese in my pocket, or anything but
the bottle of the Lagavulin whisky. And as for
the lies of John the Piper, that he will tell of me
all over the island, I will not even speak of them
to you, Miss Sheila.

It waz about fife o'clock, or maybe it waz six
o'clock, or half-past fife, and not much more
dark as if it waz the verra middle of the tay,
when I was going along by the side of Loch
Suainabhal ; and I will put my hand down on
the Biple itself, and I will sweer I waz as sober
as any man could be.   Sober indeed !—is it to be
trunk to trink a glass at a marrach ? Ay, and
many is the time I hef seen John the Piper himself az trunk that he could not find the way to
his mouth for his chanter, and all the people
laughin at him, and the wind in the pipes, but the
chanter going this way and that way by the side
of his face.   It is many a time that I will wonder
Mr. Mackenzie will let sich a man go about his
house ; and for him to speak about any one hafing
too much whisky—but I will break his pipes
ofer his head some day, as sure as Gott.   Now,
Miss Sheila, this is the whole story of it ; that the
watter in the loch waz verra smooth, and there

waz some clouds ofer the sky; but everything to
be seen as clear as the tay. And I waz going
along py myself, and I waz thinkin no harm of
any one, not efen of Aleck Cameron, that waz
away back at the farm now, when I sah something on the shore of the loch, maybe four
hundred yards in front of me, and it waz lying
there verra still. And I said to myself, "Alister,
you must not be frightened by anything; but it
is a stranche place for a horse to be lying upon
the stones." And he did not move one way or
the other way; and I stopped, and I said to myself, "Alister, it is a stranche thing for a horse
to be lying on the stones; and there is many
a man in the Lews would be frightened, and
would rather go back to Dugald MacKillop's
farm! but as for you, Alister, you will just tek
a drop of whisky, and you will go forward like
a prave lad and see whether it is a horse, for it
might be a rock mirover, ay or a black cow."
So I will go on a bit; and the black thing it did
not move either this way or that; and if I will
tell you the truth, Miss Sheila, I waz afraid of it,
for it waz a verra lonely place, and there waz no
one within sight of me, nor any house that you
could see. And this waz what I said to myself,

that I could not stand there the whole night, and that I will either be going on by the beast, or be going pack to Dugald MacKillop's farm, and there they would not belief a word of it; and Aleck Cameron, he will say I would be for going pack after him and his Campbelton whisky. And I said to myself, "Alister, you are beginning to tremple, you must tek a glass of whisky to steady yourself, and you will go forward and see what the beast is."

It was at this moment, Miss Sheila, as sure as we have to die, that I sah it mofe its head, and I said to myself, "Alister, you are afrait of a horse, and is it a black horse that will mek you stand in the middle of the road and tremple?" But I could not understand why a horse will be lying on the stones, which is a stranche thing. And I said to myself, "Is it a seal you will be seeing far away along the shore?" But whoever will hear of a seal in fresh watter: and, mirover, it waz as pig as six seals, or more az that. And I said to myself, "Alister, go forward now, for you will not hef a man like Aleck Cameron laughing at you, and him as ignorant as a child about the Lagavulin whisky."

Now, I will tell you, Miss Sheila, apout the

terrable thing that I sah; for it waz no use thinkin about going pack to the farm; and I will go forward along the road, and there waz the bottle in my hand, so that if the beast came near, I could break the bottle on the stones and gife him a fright. But when I had gone on a piece of the road, I stood still, and all the blood seemed to go out of my body, for no mortal man effer sah such a terrible thing. It waz lying on the shore—ay twelve yards or ten yards from the watter—and it waz looking down to the watter with a head as pig as the head of three horses. There waz no horns or ears on the beast; but there waz eyes bigger as the eyes of three horses; and the black head of it waz covered with scales like a salmon. And I said to myself, "Alister, if you speak, or mofe, you are a dead man; for this ahfu creature is a terrible thing, and with a bound like a teeger he will come down the road." I could not mofe, Miss Sheila; there waz no blood left in my body; and I could not look this way or that for a rock or a bush to hide myself, for I waz afrait that the terrable beast would turn his head. Ay, ay, what I went through then no one can effer tell; when I think of it now I tremple; and yet there are one or two

that will belief the foolish lies of John the Piper,
that is himself the verra trunkenest man in all
the Island of Lews.   It waz a stranche thing,
Miss Sheila, that I tried to whesper a prayer,
and there waz no prayer would come into my
head or to my tongue, and instead of the prayer
mirover, there waz something in my throat that
waz like to choke me.   And I could not tek my
eyes from the terrable head of the beast; but
now when I hef the time to think of it, I belief
the pody of it waz black and shining, but with
no hind feet at all, but a tail.   But I will not
sweer to that whatever; for it is no shame to
say that I waz trempling from the crown of my
head down to the verra soles of my feet; and I
waz watching his head more as the rest of his
body, for I did not know when he might turn
round and see me standing in the road.   Them
that sez I sah no such thing, will they tell me
how long I stood looking at him?—ay, until the
skies was darker over the loch.   Gott knows I
would hef been glad to hef seen Aleck Cameron
then, though he is a verra foolish man; and it
waz many a time I will say to myself, when I
waz watchin the beast, "Alister, you will neffer
come by Loch Suainabhal by yourself again, not

if you waz living for two hundred years or fife hundred years." And how will John the Piper tell me that—that I waz able to stand there in the mittle of the road? Is it trunk men that can do that? Is it trunk men that can tell the next morning, and the morning after that, what they hef seen? But you know, Miss Sheila, that there is no more sober man az me in all the island; and I will not pother you any more with those foolish lies.

And now an ahfu thing happened. I do not know how I am alife to be writen the story to you this day. I waz tellin you, Miss Sheila, that there waz little thought among us of sleepin for five or six nights before; and many of the nights waz verra wat; and I think it might hef been on board of the big steamer that I will get a hoast in my throat. And here, az I waz standin in the road, fearfu to mek the least noise, the koff came into my throat; and I trempled more than effer for fear of the noise. And I struggled; but the koff would come into my throat; and then thinks I, Alister, Gott's will be done; and the noise of the koff frightened me; and at the same time I tropped the bottle on the stones with the fright, and the noise of it—never will I forget the noise of it. And at the same moment the great head of the beast it will turn round ; and I could stand up no more ; I fell on my knees, and I tried to find the prayer, but it would not come into my head—ay, ay, Miss Sheila, I can remember at this moment the ahfu eyes of the beast as he looked at me, and I said to myself, " Alister, you will see Borva no more, and you will go out to the feshen no more, and you will drink a glass no more with the lads come home from the Caithness feshen."

Then, as the Lord's will be done, the stranche beast he turned his head again, and I sah him go down over the stones, and there waz a great noise of his going over the stones, and I waz just az frightened as if he had come down the road, and my whole body it shook like a reed in the wind. And then, when he had got to the watter, I heard a great splash, and the ahfu beast he threw himself in, and he went out from the shore, and the last that I sah of the terrable crayture waz the great head of him going down into the loch.

Ay, the last of him that I sah : for there and then, Miss Sheila, I fell back in the road, just like one that will be dead ; for it waz more as mortal man could stand, the sight of that terrable beast. It is ferra glad I am there waz no cart coming along the shore that night; for I waz lying like a dead man in the road, and the night it was verra dark mirover. Ay, and the fright was not away from me when I cam to my senses again ; and that waz near to the break of day ; and I was verra cold and wat, for there waz being a good dale of rain in the night. But when I cam to my senses, I began to tremple again, and there waz no whisky left in the bottle, which waz proken all into small pieces, and I said, " O Lord, help me to rin away from this water, or the stranche beast may come out again." And then it waz I set out to rin, though I waz verra stiff with the cold and wat, and I ran neither up the shores of the loch nor down the shores of the loch, but away from the watter as hard az I could rin, and ofer the moss-land and up to the hulls. It waz ferra bad trafelling, for there waz a great dale of rain fallin in the night, and there was a great dale of watter in the soft ground, and many waz the time I will go down up to my waist in the holes. But I will tell you this, Honoured Madam, that when a man haz sich a fright on him, it is not any sort of moss-

watter will keep him from rinnin ; and every
time I will stand to get my breath again, I will
think I will hear that terrable beast behind me,
and it is no shame I hef that I will be so frightened, for there waz no man alife will hef seen
sich a beast as that before.

And now I will tell you another stranche
thing, Miss Sheila, that I hef said no word of to
any one all this time, for I waz knowing verra
well they would not belief all the story of that
terrable night.   And it is this, that when I waz
rinnin hard away from the loch, just as if the
ahfu beast waz behind me, the fright waz in my
head, and in my eyes, and in my ears, and all
around me I sah and heard such stranche things
as no mortal man will see and hear before.   It
waz in the black of the night, Miss Sheila, before
the morning cam in, and it waz not one stranche
beast, but a hundred and a thousand that waz
all around me, and I heard them on the heather,
and in the peat-holes, and on the rocks, and I
sah them rinnin this way and that by the side of
me, and every moment they waz coming closer
to me.   It was a terrable terrable night, and I
waz thinkin of a prayer, but no prayer at all at
all would come into my head, and I said to

myself, " Alister, it is the tevvle himself will be keeping the prayers out of your head, and it is this night he will hef you tammed for ever and ever." There waz some that waz green, and some that waz brown, and the whole of them they had eyes like the fire itself; and many is the time I will chump away from them, and then I will fall into the holes of the moss, and they will laugh at me, and I will hear them in the darkness of the night. And sometimes I sah them chump from the one hole to the other, and sometimes they were for flecin through the air, and the sound of them waz an ahfu thing to hear, and me without one prayer in my head. Where did I rin to? Ay, Gott knows where I will rin to that terrable night, till there waz no more breath left in my body, and I waz saying to myself, " Alister, if the tevvle will hef you this night, it is no help there is for it, and you will see Borva no more, and Styornowa no more, and Uig no more, and you will never again drink a glass with the lads of the *Nighean dubh*."

I waz writen all this to you, Miss Sheila, for it is the whole story I will want to tell you; but I will not tell the whole story to the people at Borva, for there are many foolish people at

Borva, that will tell lies about any one. And now I know what it waz, all the stranche craytures I sah when I was rinnin ofer the moss—it waz only the fright in my head after I sah that terrable beast. For when I sah a grey light come into the sky, "Alister," sez I to myself, "you must turn round and look at the tevvles that are by you;" and I will tell you, Miss Sheila, that verra soon there waz none of them there at all; and I will stand still and look round, and there waz nothing alife that I could see except myself, and me not much alife whatever. But I said to myself, "Alister, the sight of the ahfu beast at the shore will turn your head, and mek you like a madman; and the stranche craytures you sah on the moss, there waz no sich thing mirover; and it is no more thought of them you must hef." And I said to myself, "Alister, you must clear your head of the fright, and you will say not a word to any one about these strange craytures you sah on the moss; perhaps you will tell your neighbours about the black horse, for it is a shame that no one will know of that terrable peast; but you will not tell them about the stranche craytures that waz on the moss, for they will be only the fright in your head." But I will tell the whole story to you, Miss Sheila; for you waz writen to Alister Lewis that I will tell you the whole story; and this is the whole story, as sure as death.

And when the grey of the morning waz cam in, I waz safe away from Loch Suainabhal; and a man is glad to hef his life; but apart from being alife, it waz little I had to be thankful for; and when the grey of the morning waz cam in, I will be near greetin to look at myself, for there waz a great dale of blood about me, for I had fallen on the side of my head on the bottle in the road, and there waz blood all about my head, and my neck, and my arm, and up to the waist I waz black with the dirt of the moss-land, and I think I could hef wrung a tub full of watter out of my clothes. Gott knows I am speaking the truth, Miss Sheila, when I will tell you I would hef giffen a shellin—ay, or a shellin and a sexpence, for a glass of whisky on that mornin; for I wazna verra sure where I waz, and the watter waz lying deep in the soft land. But sez I to myself, "Alister, you are verra well away whatever from Loch Suainabhal now, and the stranche beast he will not come out in the day-time: and now you must mek your way back to

N

Dugald MacKillop's farm." And it waz near to echt o'clock, Miss Sheila, when I will find my way back to Dugald MacKillop's farm.

And when I waz going near to the house, I sez to myself, " Alister, do you think you will go now and tell them what you hef seen about the black horse, or will you keep it to yourself, and wait, and tell the minister at Uig ? for the men about the house, now they hef been trinking, and they are not as sober az you, and they will mek a joke of it, and will not belief any of it whatever." Well, I waz not verra sure, but I went up by the byre, and I sah one of the young lasses, and when she sah me, she cried out, " Gott pless me, Alister-nan-Each ! where hef you been this night ? and it is like a madman that you are ; " and I sez to her, " Mairi, my lass, if I waz not a sober man, as you know, I would not belief myself what I hef seen this night ; and it is enough to hef made any man a madman what I hef seen this night." And she will say to me, " Alister, before you go into the house, I will bring you a pail of watter, and you will wash the blood from your face, and the dirt from your clothes ; " and I will say to her, " Mairi, you are a very goot lass, and you will mek a good wife to Colin MacAlphin when he comes back from Glasgow. Colin MacAlphin," I will say to her, " is a verra good lad, and he is not a liar, like his Uncle John the Piper ; and he does not go about the island telling foolish lies like him." That waz what I will say about John the Piper, Miss Sheila.

And when I will be going up to the house, there waz a great sound of noise, and one or two singing, and the candles inside as if it waz still the middle of the night, and I knew that these foolish men were trinking, and still trinking, and making a verra fine piece of laughing about the marrach of Dugald MacKillop and the young lass from Skye. And I went into the house, and Aleck Cameron he cries out to me, " Gott pless me, Alister-nan-Each ! and hef you not gone on to Uig, when you waz having a bottle of Lagavulin whisky with you all the way ? " And I sez to him, " Aleck Cameron, it is a verra wise man you are, but you will know not any more of Lagavulin whisky as the children about the house ; and I hef seen a strancher thing than Lagavulin whisky, and that is a great black beast that was on the shores of Loch Suainabhal, and you nor no other man ever sah such a thing ;

N 2

and it is the story of that black beast I will tell
you now, if you will gife me a glass of whisky,
for it is the worst night I hef had since ever I
will be born." Ay, Miss Sheila, there waz not
one of them will be for laughing any more when
I told them all the long story ; but they will say
to me, "Alister, it is a stranche thing you hef
told us this day, and you will go and tell the
minister of it, and Mr. Mackenzie of Borva, and
you will hear what they say about it, for there
is no one in all the island waz hearing of such a
thing before, and it will not be safe for any one
to go along by Loch Suainabhal until the truth
of it is found out, and who will find out the
truth of it like the minister, and Mr. Mackenzie
of Borva, that hef been away to many stranche
places, and gone further away az Oban, and
Greenock—ay, and away to London, too, where
the Queen lifes and Sir James himself ; and it
was a great thing for you to see, Alister, and
you will be known to all the island that you hef
seen sich a strange thing."

And then I will say to them, " Well, it is time
now I waz getting home to Borva, and Gott
knows when I will be back at Loch Suainabhal
any more, but if you will come along by the

shores of the loch, I will show you the place
where I sah the beast, and you will know that it
is true that I sah the beast." There was one or
two were for staying at home until the word
was sent to the minister; but the others of them
they had a goot tram, and they said, "Alister,
if you will be for going by Loch Suainabhal, we
will go with you by Loch Suainabhal, and we
will tek the gun that Dugald MacKillop's father
got out of the wreck of the French smack, and
if there will be any more sign of the big horse,
we will fire the gun, and he will run into the
watter again, but first of all, Alister, you will
tek a glass." And I said to them, "Yes, that
is verra well said; and we will tek the gun,
but it is not for any more whisky I am, for I
am a sober man, and there is no telling what
foolish lies they may hef about any one, for
there is ofer in Borva that foolish man John
the Piper, and every one in the island, and
Miss Sheila, too, will know that he is the
greatest one for trinking and for the telling
of foolish lies of all the people in the whole
island of Lews."

Ay, and Aleck Cameron he waz verra brafe
now, and he would be for carrying the gun, that

had the poother in it, and the flint new sharp-
ened, and the barrel well tied to the stock; but
I said to him, "It is verra well for you, Aleck
Cameron, to be brafe now, but you waz glad to
get back to the farm last night." And he is a
verra quarlsome man, Miss Sheila; and he will
say before them all, "Alister-nan-Each, I cam
back to the house pekass you waz trunk, and I
sah no black horse in Loch Suainabhal or out of
Loch Suainabhal, and you will do yourself a
mischief if you say such things about me, Alister-
nan-Each." And I will tell you this, Miss Sheila,
that it waz the foolish speech of this man, Aleck
Cameron, that gafe the hint to John the Piper
to mek a lying story about it. There is no one
more sober as me in the whole island, as you
know, Miss Sheila; and as for the trink, it waz
only a glass we had at a young lass's marrach;
and as for Aleck Cameron and his lies, did not
every one see that he could not walk in the
middle of the road with the gun ofer his shoulter,
but he waz going this way and that, until he fell
into the watter by the side of the road, and
Dugald MacKillop himself would be for tekking
the gun from him, bekass he waz so trunken a
man. I hef no patience with a man that will be

going about telling lies, whether it is Aleck Cameron or John the Piper.

Well, we waz going down the road, and there as sure as death waz the bits of the bottle that I let slip when the terrable beast turned his head, and it waz many a time we looked at the watter and along the shore, and Peter MacCombic, who is a verra frightened man, keeping to the back of us, for fear of the terrable peast. There waz no sign of him, no, for such stranche creatures, I hef been told, do not like the taylight, but only the afternoon or the evening ; and I said to Dugald MacKillop, " Dugald, there is the verra place where he waz lying." And Dugald said, " You hef seen a stranche thing, Alister-nan-Each ; and I hope no other man will see the like of it again, for it is not good to see such stranche craytures, and if I waz you, Alister, it is the minister I would be for telling."

Now, Miss Sheila, that is the whole story of the black beast that I sah, and I waz saying to Alister Lewis, the schoolmaster, " Mr. Lewis, I am not good at the writen, but if it teks me two weeks or a whole week to write the letter, I will tell the story to Miss Sheila, and she will know not to belief the foolish lies of John the Piper."

And he will say to me, " Alister, if you will be writen the letter, you will not say anything of Miss Sheila, but you will call Miss Sheila, Mrs. Laffenter, for she is marriet now, as you know, and a verra fine lady in London ; " and I will say to him, " Mr. Lewis, you are the schoolmaster, and a verra cleffer young man, but the old way is the good way, and Miss Sheila when she waz in Borva waz as fine a lady as she is now, and as fine a lady as there is any in London, and she will not mind the old way of speaking of her among the people that knew her many's the day before the London people knew her, when she waz a young lass in her father's house." And if there is any fault in it, Honoured Madam, it waz no harm I had in my head when I waz writen to you ; and if there is any fault in it, I will ask your pardon beforehands, and I am verra sorry for it if there will be any offence.

And I am, Honoured Madam,

Your most humble servant to command,

ALISTER-NAN-EACH,

but his own name is Alister Maclean.

P.S.—I waz not telling you, Honoured Madam, of the lies that John the Piper will be speaking about me, for they are verra foolish and of no consequence mirover. But if you will hear of them, you will know, Honoured Madam, that there is no truth in them, but only foolishness, for there is no one in all the island as sober az me, and what I hef seen I hef seen with my own eyes whatever, and there is no one that knows me will pay any heed to the foolish nonsense of John the Piper, *that waz trunk no further ago than the yesterday's mornin*

THE HIGHLANDS OF THE CITY.

THE HIGHLANDS OF THE CITY.

THE fairies and good people are all gone away now, and even if any of them were left, the neighbourhood of the London Exchange is about the last place in the world where one would naturally expect to find them. Nevertheless, a worthy couple living in a lane not far from the Mansion House were regularly visited each New Year's Day by an old gentleman who was quite as good as a fairy, because he invariably left a sovereign behind him; and so implicitly did they count on this visit, that on each recurrent Christmas they indulged in a few simple but unwonted luxuries knowing that the old gentleman's sovereign would pay for these. Not being philosophical persons they did not ask themselves why they ate better food on Christmas Day than on any other day; they were quite content to do as their neighbours did.

The lane in which they lived had in former

days been a place of great commercial repute ;
but now it had relapsed into dingy offices,
restaurants, and billiard-rooms, the last much
frequented about midday by young gentlemen
who were supposed by their superiors or elder
partners to be at lunch. John Holloway and his
wife and two children occupied the attic floor
of one of the tall and narrow buildings ; he was
a salesman in a boot and shoe shop in Gracechurch
Street, and these rooms were at once cheap and
handy. Now one New Year's Day, just as he
was finishing his midday dinner, and preparing
to return to the shop, some one came up the
wooden staircase and knocked at the door. His
wife was looking after the children ; he himself
answered the summons. He found before him
a stout, middle-sized, respectable-looking old
gentleman, who, as he presently discovered, spoke
with a pronounced Scotch accent. Perhaps it
was scarcely the accent that was so Scotch, so
much as the grave, earnest manner of utterance
which is characteristic of old Scotch people ;
for, as a matter of fact, the stranger frequently
and apparently unconsciously, used American
colloquialisms. It was the matter rather than
the manner of his speech which interested and

even astounded Holloway. The old gentleman looked about him for a second or two in absolute silence; then he said, in a low, deliberate way—

" You live here ? Ay, it is strange. The place is little altered. That is the outlet on to the roof, is it not ? "

He looked at a square aperture above his head, a sort of hatchway with a heavy wooden covering.

" Well, yes, it is," said Holloway, regarding the stranger with amazement.

The old Scotchman again stood silent for a second or two, looking round him in an absent way. Then he suddenly seemed to recollect himself.

" My friend, I beg your pardon. I am an old man—I forget sometimes. You were saying that the place had not been altered for years; has the roof been altered ? Is the roof still the same ? Are the ridges still there ? And the red tiles ? "

Holloway began to think that the old gentleman was a trifle off his head; but being a good-natured man he answered civilly that as far back as he knew the attics of this old-fashioned building had not been altered, and that the roof was still in ridges, and tiled. Thereupon the old gentleman—whose voice seemed to quaver at times—asked if he might be permitted to go up and out on the roof for a couple of minutes by himself. It would be a great kindness. He would gladly give Holloway a sovereign for his trouble in getting a ladder.

Holloway hesitated. There was no trouble about it; for the steps were close by; but he began to suspect that all was not right. What could be the object of any one in going out on this dilapidated old roof—on the grey and raw afternoon of a January day—with nothing visible but the backs of a lot of buildings and a bit of the side wall of the Mansion House?

All the same, he looked at the old gentleman. He did not appear to be one likely to be connected with a gang of housebreakers. In any case, what harm could be done in a couple of minutes? He would himself go up and examine the place as soon as the old gentleman had gone.

So he got the steps, removed the wooden covering of the hatchway, and assisted the stranger to ascend. In two or three minutes the old Scotchman came down again; and slipped a sovereign into Holloway's hand without speaking a word, and hurried away.

By this time Holloway ought to have been on his way back to the shop; but, just to make sure that he had done no mischief, he went out and on to the roof. Certainly there was nothing very wonderful to be seen in the scopes of tiles rising on each side to a stack of chimneys. There was no trace of the old gentleman having been there; no rope thrown over to a neighbouring building; no preparation for a burglary. He descended, told his wife of the matter, and then hurried off to the shop—puzzled, but a sovereign the richer.

Well, year by year this mysterious old Scotchman punctually paid his visit and Holloway and his wife received their sovereign, and were none the wiser. It is true they gathered several particulars about himself, for he was far from being taciturn; and once or twice, when he had brought the children some small present he stopped for a little while and talked. He was a Mr. Duncan Macnab, that they knew. They gathered from his conversation that he had been many years abroad, engaged in commerce; that his return to England had taken place just before his first visit to the lane; that he was rich; that he had but few acquaintances, and probably no relatives, for he never spoke of any. But as to the object of this annual visit no reference was ever made by him, and of course they dared not ask. But they talked about it between themselves, Mrs. Holloway being especially curious.

One New Year's Day Mr. Macnab did not arrive at the usual time; and the salesman and his wife began to look grave, for a sovereign which they had spent in anticipation was of consequence to them. Holloway waited a quarter of an hour, twenty minutes, half-an hour after the time at which he was due at the shop; then he gave up hope, and gloomily went off to his business. He had not gone five minutes when the old gentleman arrived.

Now if Holloway had been at home, his wife's curiosity would have been kept within bounds; but as it was it overmastered her courtesy, and she resolved to find out at last what this mystery was. No sooner had Mr. Macnab gone out on the roof than she stealthily crept up the steps, listening intently. There was no sound. She ventured to put out her head a little bit, and then she saw that his back was turned to her.

She could not resist the temptation to wait and see.

Yet what did she see after all ? Here was an old man standing on an old-fashioned tiled roof, and apparently lost in silence and contemplation. Then he took out from his pocket a small bottle and a glass, and she saw that his hand trembled as he filled the glass. And what was it he said— in a low and broken voice,—

"*I drink this glass to you, Ben-na-Braren; and to you, Corrie-Cranach; and to you, Ben Lena; and to any that may be alive now and near ye, and to the memory of her that kenned ye all.*"

He turned his head as he spoke, and she saw that tears were running down his face. At the same moment, too—her curiosity had spell-bound her, and she could not stir—she found him looking at her. An awful sense of guilt rushed in upon her conscience; and in some wild way she thought of standing her ground, and making an excuse; but the old man's look had nothing in it of anger or vexation at being watched. He merely said coming forward to her,—

" Take heed, my good woman, that ye do not fall."

" I—I thought—" she stammered and indeed,

as she had no excuse at all, she was forced to save herself from further confusion by simply descending the frail steps. He followed her.

The timid little woman stood before him, with her eyes cast down, as if she expected judgment to be pronounced upon her. He seemed either unaware of her indiscretion or resolved to take no notice of it.

"Where are the children, goodwife? I have some bits of things for them. Guess they don't know much about New Year's Day in this country; but sweetmeats and toys never come wrong."

The children were soon put into possession of these presents, the old man meanwhile regarding them with a strange and wistful look on his face.

"London bairns, ay," he said, apparently to himself. "The cheek white—the arms thin. But I suppose they're used to it, poor things, It is different wi' them that come from the hills —the London air tells on their cheeks, too—but that is only the first of it—only the first of it."

He turned himself from this reverie.

"Goodwife, when will your husband be home the night?"

"A few minutes after eight, sir."

Well tell him I will come down then and see him. I want him to do a bit of a job for me."

"Very well, sir."

In the evening the old gentleman came at the appointed hour ; and then it appeared his errand was to ask Holloway to take charge of a couple of flower boxes which he, Mr. Macnab, proposed to place on the roof which he had visited in the afternoon. Mr Macnab would send the boxes, have them filled up, and supplied from time to time with such plants as were appropriate to the season ; all that Holloway would have to do would be to water the flowers from time to time.

"Yes, sir, I shall be very glad to have the boxes," said he ; but he looked rather doubtfully at Mr. Macnab. He could not tell where this mania was to end.

Perhaps something in his tone or look struck the old Scotchman, who immediately said,—

"And I suppose now ye are wondering what concern I have wi' that roof o' yours. Well, it is an old story, and a long story : I thought there was no one left to care to hear it, until I saw the goodwife's head to-day peeping over the tiles, and then I knew she was curious as the rest of the women. Hoots, goodwife, there wa'nt no harm done—none at all—you go and fetch the supper in like a sensible woman, and I'll tell you the story—and I will take a glass of whisky, if ye do not mind, which I have in my pocket. It is not the first yarn I've spun in this very room, Mr. Holloway; for I was a tenant here thirty years ago. Goodwife, could you give me a drop o' hot watter?"

The story was a simple one enough; but it had its touches both of fun and of pathos; and it was garrulous and good-natured. The old gentleman did not seek to conceal the fact that as a boy his conduct had not been of the best. He was more familiar with the hills and glens— with the haunts of rabbit and blackcock and snipe—in the neighbourhood of the small Highland town in which he was brought up than with the interior of the parish schoolroom. In fact, when he did present himself before the dominie, the introduction to the day's exercises was invariably a couple of " liffies " * administered as punishment for his having played truant. More-

* Obviously from *loof*, the palm of the hand. The instrument of castigation is a good thick band of leather, sometimes divided into two tails.

over, Killietown was famous for its herring fleet; and young Macnab being a great favourite with the fishermen, they were always ready to take him off with them when they left before sunset for the night's expedition, bringing him back in the cold grey dawn much more inclined for sleep than for vulgar fractions and the reading of the New Testament. The boy's uncle, a shrewd and patient old Scotchman of the name of Imrie, who kept a shop for the sale of all sorts of ships' stores, and who was responsible for the bringing up of this incorrigible lad, knew not what to do with him. His own daughter, a blue-eyed little lass of eleven or twelve, aided and abetted the ne'er-do-weel as much as she was able, saying nothing about his playing truant, standing by him when he was found out, and sometimes even abandoning her own lessons and domestic duties to join the indolent young rascal in an excursion after blaeberries through the neighbouring glens. Of course these two became sweethearts, and young Duncan declared his bold intention of sailing away in one of the King's ships—as soon as he was old enough—and going to the countries that were filled with diamonds and jewels, and fighting and winning a heap of these that so he

might come back and make Mary Imrie his wife.
And she was quite content to wait.

In the meantime, however, Duncan Macnab
was forced to content himself with less ambitious
work. His uncle took him away from school
and wanted to apprentice him—for the lad was
tall and strong for his age—to a blacksmith.
That was no use. Duncan took as naturally to
the sea as a wild duck that has been reared by
the side of a mountain tarn. He was continually
with the fishermen. At last his uncle let him
have his will. Duncan joined a crew consisting of
four brothers who had bought a smack amongst
themselves, and then his life as a fisherman began.

So the time went on, and Duncan Macnab and
his cousin, Mary Imrie, were growing up. He,
indeed, had so far advanced to man's estate that,
in the seasons when there was no fishing possible,
he had gone to Greenock, hired himself out for a
voyage, and come back with money in his pocket.
He had not yet fallen in with the King's ship
that was to take him to the country of gold and
diamonds ; but he had found out a way of earning a livelihood, which made him independent of
his uncle ; and he worked hard, saved what he
could, and drank as little as any inhabitant of

Killietown could do. For all that, old Peter
Imrie would never look upon the lad otherwise
than as a wild, harumscarum fellow, who was
born to be a trouble to all his friends ; and at
last, when some neighbour hinted to the old
storekeeper that his daughter and Duncan Macnab were a likely-looking young couple, and
when the question was asked whether anything
was as yet settled, Mr. Imrie brought matters to
a crisis.   He told the young man to look out for
lodgings in the town, and gave him to understand
that he was not to speak to his cousin unless
when he was formally invited to the house.

This abrupt and harsh conduct bore its natural
fruit. The young people met by stealth, and
vowed, with many tears, that nothing on earth
should part them. It was the old story told
again. In recounting it over his whisky-and-
water, in John Holloway's parlour, old Duncan
Macnab seemed to be looking at a picture that
was far away. The picture was mostly of a wild
and stormy night, when the herring fleet had
thought it more prudent to remain in shelter—
the harbour of Killietown a black expanse, with
one or two points of green and red fire where
the coasters had hung up their lights—the town

visible only as a semicircle of shops, their windows blazing out into the dark—the streets
muddy and shining with the rain. Then he
could see a young fellow, not heeding the wet
very much, pacing up and down in the darkness,
and watching from time to time the lighted
doorway of one of the shops; then the muffled-
up figure of a young girl coming out; then the
hurrying away of these two to the end of the
pier, and a brief, hurried, happy interview, notwithstanding the rain and the darkness. But it
was quite otherwise on one occasion, when Duncan Macnab came home from the longest voyage
he had as yet undertaken. It was in the summer
time, for he had got back for the herring fishing;
and when he arrived in Killictown he heard that
Mary Imrie was staying with a certain Mrs.
MacDonald, a relative of hers, who had a farm
some few miles inland among the hills. Now,
the sailor lad was a great favourite with this
Mrs. MacDonald, and he made no scruple about
going straight away to the farm, and demanding
that he should be allowed to see his cousin.
Not only was that favour granted him, but the
old Highland woman also bade him rest content
at the farm for as long as he liked, seeing that

she had but few neighbours, and had seldom a stranger-face to look at. The young sailor remained at Sonachie Farm for seven long, happy summer days.

It was, indeed, a time which these two ever afterwards remembered as the happiest of their life; and there grew up in the girl more especially a sentiment of gratitude even to the inanimate objects around her—to the silent and beautiful glen, called Corrie-Cranach, where she and her lover used to wander; to the mystic solitudes of the great Ben-na-Braren, where sometimes they could descry a herd of red deer trooping quietly along the mountain-slopes; and to the more accessible Ben Lena, on the other side of the valley, which they oftentimes climbed to get a glimpse of the distant sea. Mrs. Holloway observed that whenever the old Scotchman had to mention the names of these places his eyes filled, and he paused in his speech for a moment.

Well, it was at this farm of Sonachie that these two young people made a solemn compact with each other—to this effect, that if Mr. Imrie would not listen to any reason or persuasion, they two would face the world together on their own account. That is to say, if he would not consent, they would do without his consent; and that was exactly how matters turned out. The old storekeeper said very little when he heard that Duncan Macnab had been up at Sonachic Farm; but he went himself for his daughter and marched her home; and he forbade her to leave the house for one moment without his permission. She did leave it—and for good. One wet and misty morning, Peter Imrie stood looking at a heavy-looking sloop that was just getting out of the harbour on her way to Greenock. He had been offered a share in her by the owners; and he was having a speculative look at her as the great brown sails got more and more of the wind, and the vessel became more and more dim in the rain. He did not know that both Duncan Macnab and Mary Imrie were on board that boat; though he was speedily apprised of the fact by a letter which he found on his return to the store. He made no fuss about the matter. He got another young lass to keep his accounts; and let his neighbours understand that he did not wish to talk about what had occurred.

Macnab and his sweetheart were married in

Greenock; and then the girl wrote to her father, begging his forgiveness (though she honestly declined to say that she was sorry for the step she had taken), and offering, on the part of herself and her husband, to return to Killietown, if her father would meet them on friendly terms. That letter was not answered. Then she wrote to Mrs. MacDonald, begging her to go down to Killietown, and see what could be done. Mrs. MacDonald replied that she had done so; that Mr. Imrie's answer was, that if his daughter returned to Killietown he would leave it; and that it was quite hopeless to try to make him alter his decision.

Now Duncan Macnab was a resolute, enterprising young fellow, and having patiently, out of deference to his wife's wishes, waited to see these negotiations finished, he set about making the best of existing circumstances. Moreover, the girl, too, showed high courage. She had thrown in her lot with the man whom she most loved in the world; and she was too high-spirited to confess to certain lingering lookings-back. She was not afraid. She only bargained that, until all other resources had been tried, Duncan should not go to sea; for she did not wish to be left alone in a town like Greenock, the size and noise of which bewildered her. To this Duncan replied that, as he had been able to earn a living at sea, he did not doubt he would be able to do so on land.

Good fortune generally comes to those who have the least fear of bad. The young fellow had been only three days in Greenock, making such applications for work as he could, when he ran across the owner of a ship in which he had made two or three voyages, and on this occasion the gentleman in question was accompanied by his brother, the manager of a bank in London. The latter, on hearing Duncan's story, and perhaps a bit impressed by the young fellow's frank face, said he thought he could get him a situation as hall porter to a bank in London, with 1*l.* a week, free rooms at the top of the house, and coals.

"These are the rooms we came to," said the old Scotchman at this point of the story—and there was a curious, sad smile on his face,— "this was the first house we set foot in in London."

The young Scotch girl carried her brave spirit up with her to London, resolved to make the best of circumstances, and the circumstances were not bad. Duncan's work was light enough; and he had plenty of leisure in the long evenings for educating himself, which he immediately set to work to do. Then the young wife knew little of the roar and bustle of London; she lived far above it, and it was understood that she should not descend from her Empyrean heights during office hours. Accordingly she set to make a home for herself, not only in the lofty little rooms themselves, but actually on the housetop; and there she had flower-boxes with various flowers in them; and on the quiet summer evenings, when Duncan had closed the heavy doors of the bank and gone up to his wife, that was a pleasant place for them to sit, especially as there was a stone coping to the front wall which insured their safety. And then it was that the girl, laughing at her own folly, began to make this a Highland home for herself; and that ridge of the red roof—that was the giant Ben-na-Braren; and that other ridge—that was her beloved Ben Lena, with the sea, invisible, behind it; and the hollow between, with the flowers down the centre of it—what could that be but the beautiful, silent glen of Corrie-Cranach?

In the gladness of her heart she would laugh and talk to those friends of her youth; and when she read in the afternoon it was as if she were in the still solitude of Corrie-Cranach, until the red sun in the west went down behind the Mansion House, withdrawing the ruddy glow from the • ridge of Ben Lena, and then she knew it was time to descend and prepare her husband's supper.

He grew to have as firm a faith in these fancies as herself. On high days and holidays—when the birthday of one of their distant friends came round again, for example—they invariably paid a visit to these Highland solitudes to drink a glass to the health of the absent one. But they had grown to regard the mountains and the glen as personal friends also; and the young wife—laughing, though there were sometimes tears in her eyes—never failed to say, " *And I drink to you, too, Ben-na-Braren; and to you, Ben Lena; and to you, my beautiful Corrie-Cranach; and to all that we know that are near you.*"

Now, during the progress of this story, if story it could be called, Mr. and Mrs. Holloway had noticed that the old Scotchman, who had begun in a jocular and garrulous manner, had grown more and more absent, and his talk had become disconnected. He was obviously far more engrossed with these circumstances of his bygone life than with the circumstances around him. At times it almost seemed as if he were speaking to himself. Then he ceased altogether; and his hand was playing rather nervously with the glass before him on the table.

He rose suddenly.

"Well, my friends," he said, with an effort, "that is all the story ye would care to hear. You wanted to know why I come to see ye on the New Year's Days. That is it. We were Scotch folk; we drank a glass to our friends on the New Year's Day; and when I came back again to England I thought I should like to come and see the old place—"

There was an unusual flush in John Holloway's face. The worthy salesman said, with some abruptness, "I hope, sir, you will come when you please. And there is no need to pay us money for going up above; and as for the boxes —well, you may be sure, sir, we will look after them; and if you will come every week, and

every day if you like, to see them, you will be
welcome—"

He did not seem to take much heed of this
offer; he was looking absently about the apart-
ment.

"I do not remember much now," he said
slowly, "about these rooms. They are greatly
altered; but the hills and the glen on the roof
—they are much as they were when she and I
sate there on the summer afternoons. I can
remember them—ay, better than the Ben Lena
and the Corrie-Cranach of our younger days,
that we never saw again. It is strange I will
never see them again—I had no thought I
should ever see these again. And I suppose
they have built a great house now on the side
of Ben-na-Braren; and Killietown, I hear,
has become a watering-place wi' hotels in it;
and all the old things and the old people are
gone. Well, I thank ye, friends. I did not
think to find so much remaining of what used
to be."

He was about to leave, with his sad, half-
suggested story but partly told. Somehow they
did not like to ask him questions; he was
troubled.

He preceded them to the door, and turned round with a brisker air.

" I wish ye good night. The boxes will be here in a day or two, I guess; and you will pay good heed to them goodwife—"

"Indeed I will, sir," said the shy little woman hurriedly. " But if I might make so bold, sir —you were speaking of the flowers that the young lady put up there—did she live here long ?—"

He paused for a moment.

" She lived in London, in this house, for one year and two months—and it seemed a short time to both of us. When she was dying, she said she would just like to see, only for once— but indeed there is no more of that story that ye would care to hear. Them that it concerns are all dead now, I suppose, except myself—and I shall not be long in following."

With that he abruptly turned, and disappeared down the narrow staircase. Three days afterwards the flower boxes came : they were covered over with glass, and had a few spring flowers—from a green-house, of course—in them. A few days after that again, old Macnab called on the Holloways, and had a look at the boxes ;

he was surprised to find that the flowers had not withered by that time ; but as they were evidently going, he said he would send and replace them.

After that he used to call more frequently, and made up for any trouble he might give the Holloways, by bringing or sending them presents, on various excuses. He became very friendly with them, and was blithe and cheerful in conversation ; but he never referred again to the story he had told them on that New Year's night.

This state of affairs continued till May last ; and then Mr. Macnab's visits ceased altogether. The Holloways were surprised ; they were unconscious of having given him any cause of offence ; indeed, however friendly he might be in his manner, they always treated him with great respect, and they had grown accustomed to his periodical visits. They knew his address ; and they would greatly have liked to know merely that he was well ; but it was not their place, they considered, to go visiting a gentleman who lived in Connaught Square.

At length, however—somewhere about a month after the old Scotchman's visits had ceased—a tall grave person called upon the Holloways, and asked them if they had known a Mr. Macnab. They said they had.

" The poor old gentleman," he said, "is dead. He died a few days ago, after lying for a long time in a state of insensibility which followed an apoplectic stroke. You were very well acquainted with him, were you not ? "

John Holloway merely said that Mr. Macnab had come to his house several times, and that his wife and himself had been glad to see him.

" Because," said the stranger, " he seems to have had no one about him who was familiar with his ways. He has left his fortune, which is a tolerably large one, to various institutions, with the exception of one small legacy, which falls to you. It is 50*l*. a year. There are no conditions attached ; but there is one very odd request made in connexion with the legacy. It is about that principally I have called in, to see if you understood what the old gentleman meant. He says he does not bind you by this 50*l*. to any service, but he begs of you that, as long as you remain in this house, you will look after certain flower boxes and also that on a particular evening,

which you know, you should pay a visit to
certain strange places—"

The stranger took a piece of paper from his
pocket and consulted some memoranda.

"Ben-na-Braren, and Ben Lena, and Corrie-
Cranach, which, he says, are in your immediate
neighbourhood, and that you should drink a glass
'*to the memory of her that knew them.*' This is a
very strange request. Do you understand what
it all means ? "

Apparently Mrs. Holloway did : she was
silently crying. As for her husband he said,—

" It was not necessary for the old gentleman
to have left us money to do that. We could
have done that without any money, I think."

"Well, you rob no one by taking it," continued the stranger. "Will you give me a call
in a day or two ? This is my name and address."

Since then the Holloways have faithfully
attended to the first portion of the old Scotchman's prayer. As regards the second, one may
be sure that the honest salesman will not forget,
on the afternoon of the coming New Year's Day,
to go up and drink a glass, " *To you, Ben-na-
Braren ; and to you, Corrie-Cranach ; and to you,
Ben Lena ; and to the memory of her that knew*

you." And if his wife had only some little knowledge of the Highlands, she would doubtless burst into laughter over his pronunciation of the Gaelic names ; but perhaps she will not be thinking of laughing at all just then.

LONDON:
PRINTED BY WILLIAM CLOWES AND SONS, Limited,
STAMFORD STREET AND CHARING CROSS.

The following is a complete list of the new Half-Crown Edition of Mr. BLACK'S Novels, and the probable order of their monthly issue beginning January 1892.

A Daughter of Heth. (*Ready.*)

The Strange Adventures of a Phaeton. (*Ready.*)

A Princess of Thule. (*Ready.*)

In Silk Attire. (*Ready.*)

Kilmeny. (*Ready.*)

Madcap Violet. (*Ready.*)

Three Feathers. (*Ready.*)

The Maid of Killeena. (*Ready.*)

Green Pastures and Piccadilly. (*Ready.*)

Macleod of Dare. (*Ready.*)

Lady Silverdale's Sweetheart. (*Ready.*)

White Wings.

Sunrise.

The Beautiful Wretch.

Shandon Bells.

Adventures in Thule.

Yolande.

Judith Shakespeare.

The Wise Women of Inverness.

White Heather.

Sabina Zembra.

The Strange Adventures of a House Boat.

In Far Lochaber.

The Penance of John Logan.

Prince Fortunatus.

LONDON: SAMPSON LOW, MARSTON & COMPANY, LIMITED, ST. DUNSTAN'S HOUSE, FETTER LANE.

www.ingramcontent.com/pod-product-compliance
Lightning Source LLC
Chambersburg PA
CBHW030327270326
41926CB00010B/1529